LEADERSHIP LESSONS LEARNED FROM OUR MENTORS:

Time-Honoured Values That Are Shaping the Utility Customer Experience of the Future

David J. McKendry

CS WEEK
Publishing
Sherman, Texas

Table Of Contents

FOREWORD

We all need mentors. For the fortunate, life and leadership skills training started with wonderful parents. Little else or more can outperform great parenting.

I was raised in an immigrant farming family. Both my father's parents spoke German as their primary language. Early on, my parents taught me the value of hard work. As the years progressed, I learned the true measure of their lessons. It is certainly a contrast to watch young generations embrace priorities that sometimes conflict with the lessons my grandparents and parents taught.

As you read this book, you will see the amazing influence parents and family have on children. You will also see, besides parents, other mentors and influencers who have significantly impacted how our authors developed to be individuals of substance in their communities.

I have been fortunate that my career choices offered formal, established mentoring programs which resulted in improvements in both my private and career life. These relationships produced positive results because they obliged the mentor and mentee to each other. They were based on a continuing dialog, often on a set schedule. Trust and a recognition of the wisdom and skills possessed by the mentor imparted to the mentee were foundational.

During my first job out of college as a young professional, I was assigned to a project managed by Stan Royal, a consultant from Texas. Often my harshest critic, he would not let a poorly-written sentence go uncorrected. He was formulative on many far-ranging topics like business dress and etiquette. But at the end of the day, I knew he cared about me and my family and career, and he wanted to see me succeed.

For many people, including myself, mentoring has probably been informal. People grow up and learn from experience or through simple observation of good and bad behaviors or skills. Many mentors had no idea I was watching or listening closely. In hindsight, I didn't even realize they were mentors until I later reflected on my values, inclinations, career trajectory, approach to management, interpersonal relationships and the like. Hindsight and the ability to reflect are intellectual and spiritual gifts, and they do not always arrive fast or soon. Sometimes it takes years to synthesize what was really taught and what we really learned. Informing or adjusting our future actions, words and approach are steps some take, while others may miss the point entirely.

Perhaps you have not had mentoring or coaching in your life or career. Further, you may be growing older and feel, at this point, mentoring is irrelevant, though we agree mentoring is about more than career development. For many, life aspects far outweigh any career ascension or directional correction. You might say, "You can't teach an old dog new tricks," but I disagree. In my opinion, anything you do, be it through inborne sense or habit, can be learned to perform or behave more positively.

As background, I have enjoyed a long career in consulting, mostly with PricewaterhouseCoopers (PwC) as a partner with the utilities practice. I met a great number of people across many countries and found myself asking about their careers, lives, family and development. During this multi-decade period, the airlines claim I travelled 5.5 million miles in search of helping clients. Since 1990, I have been a CS Week board and founding member and have served as its CEO since 2012.

As I think about my life and those I know, I surmised there are very few self-made people, individuals who beyond coaching and development seem to surface as wonderful people. I use the word wonderful because I feel success meets those sometimes without greatness. I know many individuals who are simply wonderful people to be around. In most cases, their work career was not a determined ascent to the top. Striving for the executive suite should not be the goal of all, perhaps but a few. When I say wonderful people, I mean those people who have achieved success in life. Career was simply an enabler to thrive in an enjoyable life. These are the people who no matter what – flat tire, bad hair, it is raining on my vacation – always seem to be happy. They freely give their time and money to others. You may know this quote: "We make a living by what we get, we make a life by what we give." — Winston Churchill.

As you read this book, you will conclude that the influence of all kinds of mentors greatly influences interpersonal development. I think the very people you know inspire us to do the right thing and be virtuous humans. In

my experience, proactive mentoring creates positive results, an[c]
tial bad mentoring can produce an understanding of negative ap[p]
life and business. Negative experience hopefully leads us to und[e]
the "trials and errors" but not to adopt them. I am acquainted
who chose to emulate bad behaviors. That tact does not bode well
run. We all need virtuous mentoring to succeed.

In the fall of 2012, I had been contemplating topics for CS We[ek]
Executive Panel. This key component of CS Week conference att[r]
audience. While screening potential topics, I think about them
time, sometimes waking at night and writing my thoughts per c[h]
get them. About then, I was lucky to be around 30-ish people wh[o]
gressing in their careers, families and marriages. I often asked t[hem]
their career development, work/life balance and other topics lik[e]
and mentoring. Their responses reinforced that perhaps we are
compass on the fine art of mentoring, and it was time to address t[he]

Alongside CS Week board member Todd Arnold, we decide[d]
an executive panel on the topic of mentoring. Titled, "Lesson[s]
Mentors (Letters I Never Wrote)," the panel was asked to tal[k]
their own photos about their mentors and forgo any PowerPoin[t]
provided them four points to discuss:

1. Key lessons learned from mentors at a young age.

2. The key lessons learned from mentors in my business ca[reer]

3. Key lessons that may have been well intentioned but fell [in]
   category of "Please don't Emulate."

4. Letters I never wrote.

The format of the panel prompted these executives to so[rt]
old childhood and early professional careers photos. While p[resenting the]
panel, we uncovered answers we expected, for example that
est mentors are parents, grandparents, relatives, teachers a[nd]
Regarding bullet 3, we were frankly worried about addressing
professional mentors who taught inappropriate lessons or pr[o]
tling lessons on how not to behave or not perform work dutie[s]

All three executives told their stories wonderfully, some e[x]
strong support, others bearing difficult losses. After the session
I talked to various attendees; all were impressed and moved b[y]
heard. I asked one which executive was the best? She answere[d]
Canadian guy; he really has a story to tell." The Canadian guy w[as]
Dave McKendry.

he mentors gone? Perhaps the connected world does
idly speaking, as I watch the social media-connected
technologically connected, but decidedly less con-
y. I log in to social media and see a superficial set of
long-term perspective, this may very well be the ele-
r all the potential great mentoring opportunities, we
eople (not just millennials) with their noses stuck to
n, engaged more with anonymous social media than
m, whether in a business or personal setting.

toring has also taken to both social media and the
rs can easily be found anywhere. But what value can
or that exists somewhere in the internet? Reviewing
hat a mentor can be hired on an informal basis. It
es not conform to basic principles of mentoring. Can
opinion? Do you respect their knowledge and skills?
als may be fictitious. Soon, they may be replaced by
If so, it will be interesting if normal conversation
ng, "My Bot just advised me on a career decision, sent
ffered me a discount on a game to play on my device.
e my brainpower." Does a true mentor charge a fee?
e fee concludes? Can a Bot be a virtuous mentor?

's chapters, I was concerned for the next generations
ctivity to people. I've put those concerns aside. My
o walk shoulder to shoulder with future generations
o invest in them.

ers heart-and-soul stories of mentors who imparted
tility leaders. Dive into these stories and see how
ht by dead people and the Greatest Generation with
vant today. I'm convinced that universal truths do
subject to derision. Their stories lay bare the truths
tion, successful relationships and how to bring out
others.

itten to be instructional, but I believe many readers
ing in the mirror and reflecting on their own devel-
s a book where the reader may grab a highlighter
gins as they read inspiring and heart-felt stories. I
hare these stories with those whom you mentor.

INTRODUCTION

Everyone has a story. Everyone has mentors who have helped shape us as individuals. In some cases, we experienced good mentors; in other cases, perhaps not so good. However we have arrived at where we are today, there is no doubt that certain individuals have influenced us along the way.

I was honoured a few years back when Rod Litke, Chief Executive Officer at CS Week, asked if I would participate in a closing panel on leadership at the annual CS Week conference. CS Week is one of the largest utility customer service gatherings in North America and no doubt the world. Started over 40 years ago, CS Week has become the premier utility customer service conference where more than 2,000 thought leaders from over 250 North American utilities convene annually to share best practices and ideas to the benefit of both our customers and our industry alike.

When Rod approached me, I was pleased to say yes – I welcomed the opportunity! However, as my talk got closer, it dawned on me that as this little chat approached, I had some serious work to do.

My wife Karen and I were fortunate to take a Caribbean cruise vacation that year. We had the special pleasure of having an aft cabin, one located at the back of the ship. It was during this down time that I took a moment to sit on a lounge chair on the back balcony of the cruise liner to collect my thoughts. There was nothing between me, the sun, the sky and the deep blue. I took out my pen and paper (yes, I went old school here). I pondered – okay, looking back over my life – who have been my mentors? What did I learn from them? I then started to jot down notes. I reflected on so many of the special people in my life starting from earliest memories to present day. Through this very cathartic exercise, I rounded out my talk. Alongside two

from Our Mentors: Time-Honoured Values That Are Shaping the Utility Customer Experience of the Future. Thank you to each and every one of you, to those who have passed on and to living mentors whom we continue to hold in such high regard.

Finally, on a personal note, I so appreciate family, friends, colleagues and acquaintances whose lives have formed the mosaic of my life, many of whom I speak of in this book. There are, however, so many others, too many to name, including bosses, peers and staff members. Thanks to each of you for the lessons I have learned. I am indeed grateful and indebted. Thank you all!

CHAPTER I

DAVID J. MCKENDRY
Senior Fellow
Canadian Electricity Association

Photo 1-1:
David J. McKendry

We all have mentors. We all have people who have influenced and guided us from the start. Sometimes, our mentors are obvious. In other cases, mentors might be those who touch our lives for a moment or a season and then move on. Mentorship might be overt and very hands on. Other times, we may simply watch and observe how others act and treat people. We learn from all these teachers. Their lessons shape us into who we are. Mentors challenge and inspire us. In the best instances, they plant in us their lessons for future generations, so these values and universal truths live long after those who taught them are gone.

The following is my story. I give thanks for all the mentors who have made such an impact on me.

I grew up in a close, loving family in a Christian home. I was an industrious kid from the start, apparently playing make-believe paperboy until I reached this lofty career goal at age eight. I delivered the *Ottawa Citizen* newspaper for five and a half years. When I look back, the business fundamentals were all there: deliver a service, deal with adversity, collect the fees owing and enjoy the rewards.

Photo 1-2: Felicity McKendry, my mother

Growing up, two very key mentors were my mother and father. My mother, now 89, was a flying instructor who started her career over 66 years ago. Prior to her retirement, she was the designated flight test examiner for the Canadian astronauts who participated in the space shuttle program. My parents met when my mother taught my father how to fly an airplane. He then went on to become an air traffic controller – so he could tell her where to go! They lived on cloud nine for 53 years until my dad passed away in 2009, having dealt with Parkinson's disease for many years.

From my mother, I learned to always be an encourager and a positive influence. She recounts often the influence of her teacher Miss Bessie Higgins. When mom was in grade five, she shyly told Miss Higgins that she would like to learn how to fly. Instead of dismissing the young girl's dream as a fantasy, Miss Higgins replied with direct eye-to-eye contact and a pointed finger added for effect, "Then some day you will!" My mother has never forgotten this key influencer in her life.

Due to her aviation background, Mom has always been a proponent of "keeping the top half of the tank full." In other words, plan ahead, consider what could go wrong and take the required action. I vividly recall her pre-flight checks as she walked slowly around the plane while closely inspecting and testing all elements of the aircraft before takeoff. She helped me formulate the process of visualizing the steps to be taken to help minimize risk.

Photo 1-3: Spence McKendry, my father

From my father, I learned that if a job is worth doing, it's worth doing right. Dad was a stickler for detail which I guess for an air traffic controller is a good thing. This mantra of doing a good job rubbed off on me. I also remember a lesson he taught in our home's basement as he was cleaning some tools borrowed from a next-door neighbour: always return borrowed tools in better shape than you got them. In other words, treat other people's property with respect, or leave things better than you found them. Just from observation, his overarching mantra was to do the right thing.

I was once told that I have my mother's spark and my father's calm disposition. If so, I am flattered and twice blessed.

Photo 1-4: James Howard Bennett, my grandfather

From my grandfather James Howard Bennett, I learned the value of service and sacrifice. My grandfather was an excellent student, but his formal education ended after he passed the examination (then required for high school) and chose to work on the family farm until 1916 when he volunteered to serve in the trenches of World War I, The War to End All Wars. Twice cited for the Military Medal (MM) for bravery, he returned from service to the family farm, determined that his children would have every opportunity to achieve their educational goals, even during the dire economic conditions of The Great Depression. I was fortunate at age 16 when he took me back to Europe to retrace his steps and to hear first-hand, gut-wrenching stories of the brave men and women who placed their lives on the line for the cause of freedom.

The same can be said for my uncle Louie Nozzolillo. Uncle Louie served in World War II as an upper and rear gunner in a Lancaster bomber. His plane was shot down over Germany on his 26th run. He parachuted, was injured and then was held as a prisoner of war for the final six months of the campaign.

Post-war, Uncle Louie married my mom's sister Connie. Aunt Connie has been another remarkable female role model for me. After earning degrees from Queen's University and the University of Ottawa, Dr. Connie Nozzolillo spent 28 years in the Department of Biology in the University

Photo 1-5: Louie Nozzolillo, my uncle

Photo 1-6: Connie Nozzolillo, my aunt

Celebrate success and give credit to the team. In Ray's world, the team members are the ones walking across the stage to receive the recognition with Ray in the front row beaming with pride. As success came with an engaged and empowered team approach, the members were the ones getting the credit, not some talking head. This simple act really drove commitment and results.

Laugh along the way. With Ray's Irish background (and he would remind you about that often), everything was done with a nod, a wink and a smile. Nothing seemed to get too serious, but if situations demanded it, everyone would sit down and work out a solution, again ending with a nod, a wink and a smile. Lesson learned: don't take yourself too seriously.

"Be an encourager and a positive influence."
– David J. McKendry

There have been other key learnings from bosses and mentors along the way:

From Larry Fox, the executive who first noticed me at Bell: capitalize on the power of MBWA – Management By Walking Around. Every month or so, Larry would drop by the sales floor from the executive suite and simply lean over the baffle and ask how things were going. This produced two results: employees were energized because 'he knows my name,' and Larry learned the latest news and opinions from the troops.

From Mike Norman, my boss's boss when I first started at Bell: continually ask yourself, do I personally have to do this, or can it be delegated? Delegate everything you can! This way, you will be able to accomplish more, and if done correctly, the person performing the work will feel empowered and valued. In other words, don't micro-manage.

I can't underscore how many great bosses I had at Bell Canada. Hugh Brownlee was a master of the plan the work, work the plan philosophy. I learned from Hugh how we could turn lemons into lemonade back in the mid-1980s. The phone company had just introduced Canada's first public electronic messaging system (aka email). Our challenge was that we shared the same problem as Alexander Graham Bell, a great technology but no one was yet on the network (remember, this was before the Internet if you can imagine!). Hugh led the planning work of how we could leverage what we did have (national associations located nearby) to fix what we didn't have (customers). Shortly thereafter, we scored a major victory by implementing a national email/database network for the Canadian Bar Association (the association of Canadian lawyers) through the introduction of CBANet. This success was replicated when we also introduced this technology in the late 1980s to the American Bar Association, which saw us running a telecommunications network for over 3,500 lawyers across the United States while we were based in Virginia. It was during this time that I also became a founding member of the United States Supreme Court Opinion Network (SCON). All of this came from planning the work and working the plan.

Mike Larkin, another Bell boss, made a huge impression on me through the power of the handwritten note, sent to the employee's home. We had just completed a major project, and although a lot of communication was being done electronically, the old school, hand-written note of thanks sent home via snail mail made a big impact. Mike really set himself apart by employing such simple tools.

Shortly after he started at Hydro Ottawa, CEO Bryce Conrad delivered a presentation to all employees through a series of meetings. In this presentation, he used many pictures, each depicting what the end goal of the corporate strategy would deliver. This presentation came complete with mocked-up, future press headlines praising the work of Hydro Ottawa. Lesson learned: start with the end in mind and illustrate it so people can visualize the goal.

I also hold many other key Bell, Hydro Ottawa and influential executives in high regard and thank them for their wisdom and belief in me. The list includes: Don Angelico, Richard Bertrand, Bill Bennett, Bruce Bibby, Bob Bose, Greg Boyle, Brian Doxtator, Mike Dunlop, Tim Edge, Joanne Fox, Peter Fraser, Phyllis Grant-Parker, Jerry Greer, Anthony Haines, Brian Hewat, Rosemarie Leclair, Marybeth MacDonald, Owen Mahaffy, Lorna Mata, John McCarthy, Jim Murphy, Andre Parker, Michel Provost, Dan Ralph, Harvey Shanefield, Al Solosky, Carol Stephenson, Ron Stewart, Al Syberg, Louis Voisine, Glain Webber and Barry Wilson.

During my tenure in the electrical utility space, I also had the pleasure of working for Norm Fraser. Norm is a great believer that you can't manage what you can't measure. Norm was an excellent role model in determining what and how to measure progress through appropriate Key Performance Indicators (KPIs).

Not all my bosses have been great ones, but for those unnamed, I still appreciate the following key lessons learned:

It's not about looks; it's about substance. The nice suit may look good, but substance and caring for people will go much further.

It's not about win/lose; it's about win/win. I once had a boss who only seemed concerned with the side he was playing on. I have found this approach very short-sighted because you may win the battle, but you will likely lose the war. Instead, strive to achieve results for both parties when negotiating a deal. This will set you up for success in the long run.

People don't leave jobs; they leave their bosses. Sometimes the worst jobs can be made tolerable by the environment created by the boss. I love Richard Branson's quote, "Train people well enough so that they can leave, treat them well enough so they don't want to." In essence, equip others so they can be all they can be.

"Do what you say you are going to do." – David J. McKendry

From all these mentors and unnamed others, I've learned additional key lessons including:

Do what you say you are going to do. So often, hopes and plans get dashed when someone you are relying on doesn't follow through on promises. This simply does not bode well for building trust and relationships.

Show up on time. Not showing up at the appointed time is disrespectful to those that have made the effort to join at the agreed to hour. I learned from others how effective it can be to simply close the door on a meeting room shortly after its start time and proceed without those who were late.

Communicate the good, the bad, the ugly. So often, issues arise when communication stops. The sign of a healthy relationship, be it at home or at work, is an environment where trust allows all things to be communicated, even the bad news. It is best for all when communication channels are open, and trust abounds.

Don't let things fester. Fess up. This lesson ties in with the concept of fostering an environment with open communication. Sometimes, we may feel nervous about letting others know that we messed up. It is best, however, to share what happened, and be sure to explain how you plan to fix the issue.

The truth is always the best path to take. Don't lie. It is never the best path. Full stop.

Say please and thank you. Perhaps some of you have experienced a boss or co-worker who doesn't have the courtesy to say these magic words. It is amazing the respect that is garnered by simply showing your respect and gratitude.

Honey will get you further than vinegar. It may sound trite but being kind in a work environment will produce significantly better results and gain the admiration of the team. Roger Marsh, a colleague with whom I have worked for a number of years, has a great saying, "Be tough on the issues and easy on the people." Roger has gained much respect not only for what he does, but also for how he accomplishes it.

Hold regular meetings with staff and ask for their input. Regularly scheduled one-on-one meetings are an excellent way to step back from the daily grind to work "on" the business away from the ongoing distractions of being "in" the business. Have each participant (including yourself) come to the meeting prepared with a short list of topics to discuss. This keeps the conversation focused and is a good reminder of things to be dealt with later, if time doesn't permit now. This ongoing two-way communication builds trust amongst the team while driving forward motion and a record of ongoing accomplishments.

Help others get what they want, and they will help you get what you want. This is an old axiom that is worth remembering because it works.

People don't care how much you know until they know how much you care. This is a great phrase by noted leadership author and speaker John Maxwell. Truth is indeed simple.

Don't respond in haste. Sleep on it. Too often we can tend to respond in the heat of the moment and say or write something that we might regret later. Like time, regrettably, a second thing that we cannot reverse is words said, and the tongue is indeed sharper than the sword. In many cases, it is better to sleep on it and respond the next day with a clearer mind.

Be humble. I have watched my father-in-law Roger Moyer with admiration. He is considered by many to be wise beyond measure; however, he operates from a position of humility and with a servant's heart.

Be thankful. People tire easily with complaining and statements of how bad things are. Step back and consider all opportunities and blessings. Be thankful and remain positive.

Be genuine. Anyone can see through a fraud. Be genuine with everyone you encounter.

Listen. God created us with two ears and one mouth, and they should be used in that proportion. Too often, we can tend to talk over each other. We may not be truly listening. Avoid preparing your response while the other person is talking.

Employ three powerful words, "Help me understand." This was a favourite saying of a wonderful friend and work colleague that I greatly admired. Roy Chapman found that this simple phrase was much more effective and inclusive than telling others that they were doing things wrong. Sadly, Roy lost his life way too early in a tragic accident.

The most important question that a leader can ask is, "How can I help?" This basic question (with appropriate follow-through) from a boss to a subordinate greatly reduces stress and opens the lines of communication. Give it a try!

If people didn't make mistakes, pencils wouldn't need erasers. I love this catch-phrase from Richard Latulippe, a human resources colleague of mine who learned it from one of his mentors. So many times, we find ourselves in a state of 'paralysis by analysis' because we fear making a mistake. At other times, we fear the repercussions after we have made a mistake. The point here is that we should encourage people to try a task and to accept mistakes as part of the process because we all make them.

Praise in public; discipline in private. When there is good news to share, build up the team and the responsible individuals publicly. When a matter needs to be addressed to improve a behaviour, it is much wiser to do it privately behind closed doors.

Treat people the way you would like to be treated,
especially if you're the boss. – David J. McKendry

Give the credit and take the blame. Lance Jefferies, a wonderful colleague who is Hydro Ottawa's Chief Electricity Distribution Officer, reminded me of this great credo. A leader who is humble enough to give the credit to others, while backing the team by taking the blame when things don't turn out as planned, will earn considerable trust. Lance consistently serves as a great role model of this practice.

Catch people doing things right. So often people are blamed for things that go wrong. At times, it might be the truth; however, it is much more uplifting, invigorating and inspiring to a team when you can demonstrate this phrase with action. This simple move helps to reinforce desired behaviours and makes for an enjoyable work environment.

Don't be afraid to step forward to make things better. Life is a series of decisions and resulting consequences. Sometimes, it is up to you to decide and take the steps necessary to make things better.

Lead from where you are. If you think you're too small to have an impact, remember the power of a mosquito in the room when you are trying to sleep!

Don't get discouraged as you take on leadership roles. Don't be downcast if things aren't progressing as quickly as you think they should be. If a door doesn't open, it may not be your door... for now.

Left foot, right foot. Sometimes, a "left foot, right foot" approach to progress is called for because every journey starts with a single step. Keep learning, and don't try to run a sprint every day. Remember, you are in a marathon called life.

People are like string. Jamie Beavis, a colleague of mine, tells the story of a mentor who explained to him that people are like string. Jamie's mentor then proceeded to demonstrate by placing some string on the table, "If you push the string, it gets all tangled and bunched up. However, if you lead the string, it will follow. The same holds true for people. Don't demand, instead lead."

It's not the hard skills and soft skills, it is the hard skills and the harder skills. I was recently educated on this maxim by Alan Kearns of CareerJoy. When discussing the difference between the traditional hard skills, i.e. technical skills needed to carry out a job, versus the soft skills like people management skills, Alan suggested (with years of experience dealing with people under his belt) that the reference should actually be to the "hard" skills and the "harder" skills. His rationale favours the latter because, in many cases, people management can be more difficult to master than the technical skills required for a particular job.

Exceed customer expectations one customer at a time. I attribute this phrase to Sid Ridgley of Simul Corporation, a trusted voice of reason on all things customer. Sid is right. It is hard to right a ship or to build Rome overnight. Sometimes change must take place over time by serving each customer exceptionally well, one at a time.

Open-ended questions foster innovation. By asking open-ended questions such as, "Why do we do things this way?" or "Is there a better way?" or "Can you please help me understand…?" or "How can I assist?" you will find that team members will start to explore new options and will draw their own conclusions on how to make things better.

Be mindful of voice and posture. A loud voice can be intimidating as can a shoulders-back, barrel-chested stance, especially if the sender encroaches on the receiver's personal space. Be aware of how you are physically positioning yourself and be respectful of the other person. A soft voice along with a relaxed stance at an appropriate distance will help get the job done.

Read books and literature. The written word holds a wealth of leadership wisdom. From the Bible to Dale Carnegie's *How to Win Friends and Influence People*, books have provided significant guidance to me. Recently, I have been reflecting on the impact of the famous poem, *If* by Rudyard Kipling. This poem was framed and hung in my bedroom as a boy, and it remains on the wall in our home to this day. When talking about leadership lessons, there are many key takeaway points in Kipling's prose. Penned in 1895, the words are as relevant today as they were well over a century ago.

If
Rudyard Kipling

If you can keep your head when all about you
Are losing theirs and blaming it on you;
If you can trust yourself when all men doubt you,
But make allowance for their doubting too;
If you can wait and not be tired by waiting,
Or, being lied about, don't deal in lies,
Or, being hated, don't give way to hating,
And yet don't look too good, nor talk too wise;

If you can dream – and not make dreams your master;
If you can think – and not make thoughts your aim;
If you can meet with triumph and disaster
And treat those two impostors just the same;
If you can bear to hear the truth you've spoken
Twisted by knaves to make a trap for fools,
Or watch the things you gave your life to broken,
And stoop and build 'em up with wornout tools;

If you can make one heap of all your winnings
And risk it on one turn of pitch-and-toss,
And lose, and start again at your beginnings
And never breathe a word about your loss;
If you can force your heart and nerve and sinew
To serve your turn long after they are gone,
And so hold on when there is nothing in you
Except the Will which says to them: "Hold on";

If you can talk with crowds and keep your virtue,
Or walk with kings – nor lose the common touch;
If neither foes nor loving friends can hurt you;
If all men count with you, but none too much;
If you can fill the unforgiving minute
With sixty seconds' worth of distance run –
Yours is the Earth and everything that's in it,
And – which is more – you'll be a Man, my son!

Photo 1-11: Don Bertrand, my dad's boss and mentor

As I mentioned, my father was an air traffic controller. He recounted a story that stuck with me about one of his bosses, a fellow named Don Bertrand. In 2008, I heard that Mr. Bertrand, then in his 90s, was dealing with cancer and didn't have long to live. I decided to look up Mr. Bertrand. I found his number and called. His son-in-law answered. I explained the situation, and he put his father-in-law on the phone. "Yes, son, what can I do for you?" my father's former boss asked in a strong voice. I explained that I was Spence McKendry's son, and I was calling to say thank you. "Thank you for what, son?" I explained that my father had told me a story that meant a lot to him, and it had to do with his mentor whom I was now speaking with decades later. "What story is that, son?" I recounted that my father overshot an airplane; in other words, he made the pilot take another circuit before landing due to some interruption on the runway. The pilot was upset and after landing called Mr. Bertrand to complain. My father overheard Mr. Bertrand explain to the pilot on the phone, "The controller did what he thought best at the time." He hung up the phone, turned to my dad and then quietly said, "So what happened?" There was no major issue. The point that my dad took away was: stand by your team, and they will stand by you. As we ended our conversation, I explained to Mr. Bertrand that I listened to this lesson and have tried to apply it to my career, and for this I thanked him. He paused and thanked me for calling. He told me it meant a lot to him. Mr. Bertrand died shortly thereafter. Lesson learned: let people know how much you appreciate them in the living years.

I was fortunate to be able to spend the last week of his life with my father and to express my gratitude to him. With others such as Coach O'Brien, Mr. Brooks, Larry Fox, and Roy Chapman, I missed the opportunity as they each died suddenly at relatively young ages. Lesson reinforced: Let people know how much you appreciate them in the living years.

So, there you have it, some of the lessons learned from my mentors. I am sure that you have many more to add to my list. I would encourage you to take the time to list all the people who have been an influence in your life, be it positive or negative and write down what you learned from these individuals. Two key takeaways stand out: mentorship lessons span across generations and be sure to continually reach out in the living years to those who have been an influence on you and say thank you. I guarantee that it will be a rewarding experience for both you and those for whom you are thankful.

After reflecting on my mentors, my interest in learning others' leadership lesson stories was sparked. I have continued to seek out mentors and people who can be positive influencers on my life. For example, I have relished the opportunity to know Todd Arnold, a fellow CS Week Board Member. Todd has willingly listened to some of my challenges, and I have greatly appreciated his wisdom. Todd is an excellent reminder that it is not only **what** we do in leadership roles, but **how** we do it. In many cases, the how can be as important, if not more so, as the what.

Another example is Penni McLean-Conner, Chief Customer Officer and Senior Vice President Customer Care of Eversource and CS Week Board Chair. Penni's enthusiastic, can-do attitude is contagious. It is no surprise that she has risen to the top in the utility sector, and I appreciate her being a strong influence on me. I am especially honoured that both Todd and Penni agreed to be co-authors in this book.

Read on and be inspired by many other leadership lessons learned from mentors. Through the sharing of over 2,000 years of collective experience from those who have successfully risen through the professional ranks in the utility sector across North America, you will learn the qualities of great leaders. You will also learn lessons on how to build trust while fostering the future, solutions, strategy, planning, motivation, excellence, success, quality and innovation. Enjoy!

David J. McKendry is Senior Fellow with the Canadian Electricity Association (CEA) and a former Director Customer Service at Hydro Ottawa. The CEA is regarded as the National Voice of the Electricity Industry in Canada. Hydro Ottawa Limited, the third largest municipally-owned electrical utility in Ontario, Canada, serves more than 330,000 customers.

CHAPTER 2

TODD ARNOLD
Senior Vice President (Retired)
Duke Energy

Photo 2-1: Todd Arnold

Thinking through over 50 years of serving customers gives me an opportunity to remember so many wonderful people that had a positive impact on my career. Even though I am only sharing a few stories here, I was blessed to work with countless special people who gave the gift of their experience and wisdom.

I know it is typical to name your parents as one of your key mentors. The same is true for me as I was blessed with great parents. But my father's mentoring went beyond the normal parent lessons because he was also my business mentor. For over 30 years, my father owned and operated Arnold's Newsstand on the courthouse square in Sullivan, Indiana. I describe it as a drug store without the drugs or a convenience store before the days of convenience stores. During a time when most businesses were only open 9 to 5 and closed on Sunday, Arnold's Newsstand was open from 6 am to 8:30 pm, 365 days a year. If you needed coffee, cigarettes, newspapers, bread, milk, film (yes – photos were on film not your phone), batteries (devices weren't rechargeable) and

Photo 2-2: Arnold's Newsstand, Sullivan, IN

flashbulbs (Google it), or you needed to catch up with your social network (pre-internet/Facebook/Twitter), you went to the Newsstand because it often was the only place open within 25 miles.

Somewhere in my single digits of age, I began working behind the counter serving Newsstand customers. During my high school years, I was opening the store at 6 am and doing the payroll and accounting. It wasn't until many years into my utility career that I realized my love for business and serving customers came from all those hours behind the counter with my Dad. While most boys were playing sports with their fathers, I was waiting on his customers. People often thought I was a workaholic with no hobbies. What they didn't realize was that my hobby was thinking about business and serving customers because that was the equivalent of playing baseball with my father.

The lessons I learned were endless. The customer is always right. Greet customers with a smile and never forget to say, "Thank you!" Don't be shooting the bull when a customer is waiting to be served (something forgotten in too much of today's retail). And don't park your own car on the courthouse square near his business. Those spots were reserved for the paying customers. I could go on and on. Frankly by themselves, they're not earth-shattering lessons. But by the hundreds they build the basic foundation for delivering great customer service. And that's what's missing today – understanding the basics. Yes, we've seen a flood of new technologies and channels for serving customers. But the basics have not changed.

"Greet customers with a smile and never forget to say, 'Thank you.'" – Todd Arnold

---

The main advice I'd give others from the years with my father behind the counter is that you must find times in your career that you get to serve your customers directly. And the earlier the better. Too many people leading businesses today have never served customers face-to-face or worked directly with those who do. There is not a more important classroom than directly serving those who pay your salary. Find ways to be close to your customers and to those who serve your customers directly.

As for my corporate career mentor, I was lucky to get to work for one who is universally regarded as the greatest leader in that company. I won't mention his name here because it would embarrass him. But those who worked in the 1980s and 1990s for PSI Energy/Cinergy would easily guess who I am referring to. Read any book on great leaders, mentoring leaders, servant leaders…. and you will see the embodiment of this person.

As his career grew, I was fortunate he saw strengths in me that I didn't see in myself and therefore, I got to grow my skills working for him in many different roles. I was fortunate to have many good, and not so good, leaders to learn from. But this particular leader had the greatest impact on my career going from an entry position of energy consultant to Senior Vice President with Duke Energy.

"You must find times in your career that you get to serve
your customers directly. And the earlier the better."
– Todd Arnold

One of his critical skills was finding people with potential and giving them opportunities to grow and excel. He "walked the talk" when it came to the proper way to treat people and instilled those values throughout the organization. He also would make the tough decisions that were best for the organization. That's why some of the most important lessons I received from him came when I thought I had been screwed. Keep in mind this person selected me numerous times for great opportunities, often ahead of others who thought they deserved them. But there were two times he made major reorganizations that diminished my responsibilities.

In the personal hurt, pain and anger, I learned some important lessons. A great leader has to make tough decisions that won't make everyone happy. The boss, like any great coach, must play the best players and that might not include me. If I was to be a good leader, I had to be prepared to make unpopular decisions.

And maybe the greatest lesson was the value of keeping your mouth shut as you go through the natural stages of grief of career disappointments. I had seen others damage their careers by sounding off to everybody around them about how the boss had shafted them. As much as you might want to vent, don't! Keep your chin up, carry on and play through the pain. I learned that great careers, even when working for the greatest of mentors, are not linear. They have highs and lows and how you respond is the most import-ant determinant of your overall career trajectory.

I'll end with what I think are the most undervalued mentors – books! Throughout my career I was reading books that paralleled the challenges in my career. Through books, I had the smartest people in the world speaking directly to me and guiding me along the way.

"A great leader has to make tough decisions that won't make everyone happy." – Todd Arnold

---

Often the words on the pages became a North Star to guide me throughout my career. One such passage came from a 1991 book titled, *Love and Profit: The Art of Caring Leadership* written by James Autry who was president of a major publisher of top-selling magazines. In his introduction, he provided me with the best description of leadership that I have ever read. He uses the vernacular of the day, "management," for what we call leadership today.

Autry says, "Management is, in fact, a sacred trust in which the well-being of other people is put in your care during most of their waking hours. It is a trust placed upon you first by those who put you in the job, but more important than that, it is a trust placed upon you after you get the job by those who you are to manage."[1]

Autry goes on to provide a challenge which I took to heart and encourage you to do the same, "Approach management as a calling, a life engagement that, if done properly, combines technical and administrative skills with vision, compassion, honesty, and trust to create an environment in which people can grow personally, can feel fulfilled, can contribute to a common good, and can share in the psychic and financial rewards of a job well done."[2]

Having retired, I'm now entering that phase of life where my best mentors are my grandchildren. They teach me to find joy in all things. I wish the same for you.

Todd Arnold, now retired, is a member of the CS Week Board of Directors. He is a utility industry veteran with over 40 years of experience, author of the book, *Rethinking Utility Customer Care, Satisfying Your Always-Connected, Always-On Customers*, and served as senior vice president, smart grid and customer systems with Duke Energy, as well as senior vice president, customer service.

---

1   Autry, James A., *Love and Profit: The Art of Caring Leadership.* New York: William Morrow and Company 1991, p. 15
2   Ibid, p. 13-14

CHAPTER 3

FRANCIS BRADLEY
Chief Operating Officer
Canadian Electricity Association

Photo 3-1: Francis Bradley

Teachers play an enormous role in the lives of their students. I was lucky to engage with two who taught lessons that influenced me in high school and college and still inform me today. In high school, the teacher who taught twentieth century world history, was one. At first, I thought his class dull, but as time and the subject progressed, I began to realize my teacher shared more than words on a dusty page. I made it a point to ask him some questions before and after class which led him to tell me that he was a displaced person at the end of World War II. His classroom stories of DP camps talked about individual people from his first-person perspective. His experiences were tactile and sensory as he shared what it was like to live as a homeless person in a succession of unsafe places that were scary and temporary. He longed for a safe home. Hearing his experiences, it made me appreciate that everyone has a story and everyone's stories are different. It also had me wondering further about my dad's experiences in WWII. I talked to my mother about my teacher and my wonderings. This, along with interest from me and my siblings, spurred her to interview my dad and document all his WWII stories for the family. She assembled and published his memoirs, "Charlie's War," for the family, and my brothers and sisters and I have them now as a legacy to share his history with our children. Riches come from these stories and taking the time to understand and appreciate them has, in turn, enriched my family.

> ## "While words are meaningful, they are made more so when backed by action." – Francis Bradley

---

The second teacher, Bob Keaton, taught political science at Dawson College in Montreal, where I attended. Very politically active and co-founder of a municipal political party, Mr. Keaton believed that while words are meaningful, they are made more so when backed up by action. Late in the 1970s, the city of Montreal raised a plan to change its official coat-of-arms. A French trading post more than three hundred years ago, Montreal had grown into a large, cosmopolitan city, and elected officials wanted to reflect that growth and expansion by updating the city crest to something modern or at least what was considered modern by 1970 standards. Its historical coat-of-arms, adopted in 1833, had featured four symbols: the French fleur-de-lis, the English rose, the Irish clover and the Scottish thistle; each representative of major ethnic groups who built the city. Hearing that the historical crest was under attack, Keaton's sensibilities were offended, and he along with many friends and colleagues, not to mention students influenced by his classroom lectures, were inspired to take this protest to the streets. Keaton felt the new coat-of-arms turned its back on the rich cultural diversity that had built the city. We started petitions to gather public opinion and signatures. As his supporters, we spent a lot of time wearing down shoe leather and following his example that actions speak louder than words. I recall one day spending hours in front of the Olympic stadium during a baseball game, not attending the game but getting signatures on a clipboard that offered two images: the old and the new. Anywhere there was a crowd, we would gather with our clipboards, pens and images of the coat-of-arms options. I had to answer questions on the spot. I was a young adult respecting history. I saw the power of people behind an idea. Our efforts were successful. The change initiative was defeated, and the original coat-of-arms remains Montreal's proud symbol of its multi-cultural heritage, the only change being the addition last year of a white pine symbol, recognizing Indigenous Peoples as one of the five founders of the city.

After classroom teachers, the most influential mentor during my business career certainly was Hans Konow. When he first hired me at the Canadian Electricity Association in 1986, Hans was the manager of public affairs and I was his most junior team member. I often joked to Hans that either I had to push him up the ladder ahead of me or I'd have to kill him. I'm glad to report I did the pushing, and he did the climbing. Hans eventually became president and CEO of CEA, and the Board of Directors selected me to serve as Vice President. So, we moved lockstep together, with our successes built upon a relentless focus on our members. Our purpose: to understand what our members wanted. Our mission: to craft programs and services that met or exceeded our members' expectations. The difference with Hans was his belief that you couldn't appreciate those member "wants" until you walked in their shoes. Hans wanted our team out in the field. He encouraged site visits. He pushed us to meet our members at their facilities, in their offices, on their turf. Only by "walking in their shoes" could we understand the context for the work we performed on our members' behalf.

"I saw the power of people behind an idea."
– Francis Bradley

Today, as the Chief Operating Officer of CEA, I stick to the basics learned from Hans. Perhaps my direct reports are sick of hearing this, but I can't repeat the message often enough: We can't be successful as a national association if we try to do it from our office in Ottawa. Rather, we need to go to their offices, job sites, conferences, visit their facilities and fully immerse ourselves in our members' context. With that shared understanding, we can succeed together.

Over the years, I have watched national association CEOs try to lead from their central office. Those CEOs don't last, and often don't understand why their Boards release them. It's simple: they've lost touch with their members. When I was named COO, I made sure we ran the association with the lessons Hans taught.

The other day, one of my direct reports proudly showed me a boxful of swag from Oakville Hydro, the local distribution company of a Toronto suburb ranked as the 15th best place to live in Canada. The Oakville Hydro team was so pleased that CEA staff had visited and spent the better part of a day listening to concerns and learning from the perspectives of a local electricity company that they showered him with company-branded mousepads, pens and a mini drone to fly around the office! It's such a simple thing: spend time with your customers and get to know them. Our members are our customers at CEA.

"Spend time with your customers and get to know them."
– Francis Bradley

Before coming to work at CEA, I worked for someone I will respectfully call a "data worshipper." Numbers, statistics, analytics: these drove his belief in using public opinion polling results to gain insights and craft marketing and communications strategy. When I joined CEA, one of my responsibilities was to set-up and run CEA's customer opinion and research program. I found that while surveys were important and useful, it was at the focus groups where we gained real insights. We learned that while studying customer satisfaction survey data is important, those numbers don't tell a customer's story. Rather, we found focus groups, hearing individual voices, were the most reliable medium for harvesting customer sentiment. Studying customer satisfaction was useful, but that didn't represent the voice of the customer. This led me full circle back to my members who don't neatly translate to numbers on a spreadsheet. While we could group them in various ways, these individuals have their own stories and hold their own beliefs, just like my high school history teacher and Professor Keaton. Our customer insights were honed by digging into the individual stories these people told and why they felt favourably or unfavourably about electricity companies. While he understood the use of statistics and metrics, my earlier "data worshipper" missed the most important part of the formula: people as individuals. This realization created a "eureka" moment for me, making me appreciate some of the work done by Dave McKendry of Hydro Ottawa and others who have extensively studied personas and tried to understand customer similarities and aggregated experiences.

If I could write a letter to my mentors, it would be short and sweet. I would thank my high school history teacher for making me want to see the world. I would thank Bob Keaton for making me want to change the world. And, I would thank Hans for giving me the opportunity to try to do both.

Managing daily operations, overseeing the Councils, Committees and Task Groups and leading company security activities, Francis Bradley is the Chief Operating Officer of the Canadian Electricity Association. CEA is the national voice for safe, secure, and sustainable electricity for all Canadians, and provides its members with value-added products and services to advance the strategic interests of Canada's electricity industry. CEA addresses those needs and diverse interests of its 35 members while working closely with its corporate and associate partners.

CHAPTER 4

SANDRA BROUGHTON
Director, Customer Experience
Southern Company Gas

Photo 4-1: Sandra Broughton

Three women shaped my thinking during childhood's formative years: Nellie, my maternal grandmother; Julia, my mother; and Carrie, my paternal grandmother.

Bold, self-confident and brave, Nellie B. Wiggers Robinson knew no master. She was bold and courageous. She helped my grandfather work his farm. I literally saw her chase cows and chickens and pigs. She knew how to drive the tractor or steer the wagon or change the car tire. She could till the ground; her vegetables were among the best in the county. She freely gave to others, helping those in need. She organized the women and dialogued openly with men. Her laughter rang out, infectious to those who heard it. My grandfather treated her as his equal. She had strengths and skills that he didn't. He preferred that she drive the car while he sat on the passenger side. She didn't back down from hard work. Together, they raised three strong sons and a daughter. Nellie taught my mother strong ethics and taught me the same. I spent time with her in the summers or Thanksgiving or Christmas holidays.

Photo 4-2: My grandmothers Nellie and Carrie with my mother Julia in 1972

She gave me tasks she knew I could handle but also challenged me. She gave me books to read, encouraged me to dream and learn as much as I could. She supported my goals, celebrated my successes and rewarded me with favor and gifts and money. She taught me faith through evening Bible study, time spent in prayer and Billy Graham and sometimes Oral Roberts crusades. We rode to church together. She encouraged me to never waste my time and to be active. Time spent with her was always full of schedules and meetings, duty and chores. She worked hard, much of it manual. She overcame it all and excelled.

Photo 4-3: Julia, my mother

My mother, Julia M. Robinson Hayes is amazing, the original multi-talented, multi-tasking creative life force that ran our family and ensured the success of our moderate-income, eight- person (father, mother, four sons and two daughters) household. While Daddy held down two full-time jobs and a personal business, Mama organized, coordinated, commanded and orchestrated the household. She taught me that I could do and be anything I wanted to do and be. She taught us all how to make something out of very little. Mama's reading material was any "how to" instructions. The house was full of dictionaries, encyclopedias, recipe books, instruction manuals and Bibles, plus all kinds of stuff she constructed. She built furniture, designed fashion, canned vegetables and created quilting masterpieces among the myriad of artistic and practical things she mastered. Mama stretched budgets, fostered musicianship, developed talent and embraced diversity in our home and our community. She and my father, age 84 and 88 (at the time of this writing), enjoy a healthy, interdependent lifestyle living on their own without assistance. Mama insisted that I do my best and that I continue to improve. She modeled that behavior. I watched her take on one growth challenge after another during my lifetime. If she wanted to do it, she learned how to, and then she did it. Without fail, she persevered, learning from mistakes, adjusting

Photo 4-4: My family

the plan and getting the results she wanted. Love and respect cannot adequately describe my admiration for the phenomenal woman she is. She often walked throughout our house praying for our family, asking for wisdom and guidance to be the best person she could be and seeking the same for those around her.

Carrie Childs Hayes, my paternal grandmother, brought the softer side to this trio of women. She was a quiet, resolute woman of strength and solitude. Life had been challenging for her, having lost her mother as a young child and helping raise a younger sister as she herself grew up. Her daddy, a gospel preacher, lived by the Word. Grandma Carrie gave me my first book of children's Bible stories. It told of the heroes of faith like Joseph and David, Jonah and Mary. These stories, edited for a child's perspective, not only shaped my imagination of their courageous exploits but also solidified my faith in a power that created the universe and took care of everything in it. As my grandmother walked out her life of faith for 91 years, she remained humble and kind, resourceful and reconciling. She endured patiently and taught our family to love one another.

"Without fail, she persevered, learning from mistakes,
adjusting the plan and getting the results she wanted."
– Sandra Broughton

Those three influential and faith-led women influenced me profoundly, but others had an impact too. Glenn Randall was my favorite high school math teacher. He had a long, effective career of more than 40 years with the Atlanta Public School system. I was his student during the early years while attending Walter F. George High School. Mr. Randall loved math. He inspired me to love math too. He taught me to use my imagination when solving word problems. He took time to sit, side by side, coaching students until the concept was mastered or at a minimum understood. Mr. Randall had a sense of humor and never seemed bothered by the antics of my classmates. If they acted silly, he said something funny to correct them, and we'd continue with class. He didn't allow his patience to break. But, he would let the students know when a line was crossed. He'd lose the humor and become really stern. I was fascinated to grasp how numbers worked, algebra, trigonometry and so forth. Those classes were the beginning of my analytical life journey, working through word problems and complex equations. I was disappointed whenever his absence brought a substitute to our class. After his retirement, Mr. Randall continued to help students through APS' tutoring program. For more about Mr. Randall, here are a couple of links:

- *Atlanta Journal Constitution* feature (http://www.ajc.com/ news/local/sunday-conversation-with-glenn-randall/ ZXzjqzalFaM4tuXfHhorwN/)

- Award winning homework hotline (https://talkupaps.wordpress. com/2011/01/25/aps-award-winning-homework-hotline-answers-students-questions/)

"He took time to sit, side by side, coaching students until the concept was mastered or at a minimum understood." – Sandra Broughton

---

Photo 4-5: One of my earliest professional mentors, Fredric A. Stanley

Once I left school and entered the work-force, at least four other mentors shared their time, experience and lessons with me. The first, Fredric A. Stanley taught me to take risks. I served as his executive administrator in an organization in need of change. He was fearless and rushed in to face challenges or obstacles in his way. While his approach was dynamic, some thought him reckless and possibly ill-pre-pared. I knew him contrary to that. Actually, he was a man of deep thought and conviction. He studied tirelessly and calculated risks. He looked at what-if scenarios and weighed pos-sibilities before he moved. These things were done with sensitivity, and he often cried. But he was willing to take the risk and to possibly lose. He often said he was preparing me for the day I'd take over for him, insisting that I pay attention. He was the first manager I had that performed a daily check in, like clockwork, going over yesterday's results and what to expect today. He always asked my opinion and worked to reconcile where our opinions differed. He taught me leadership trust. At times he'd go with my opinion and defer his own, even when he knew better. I later realized he was setting up lessons-learned opportunities. I also realized he would have a recovery plan. He was my greatest mentor. I mentioned earlier that some thought him to be reckless in his actions. He was not reckless but didn't always explain to others exactly what was happening and why. Once he decided to act, he moved quickly, without pause. His endeavors, though quite successful, were often uncelebrated because he moved in that way. One of his favorite quotes was, "I want to sit where the people sit." Ironically, it meant he wanted to have compassion and connect with those he led. Yet, his action style did not always display those sentiments. Unfortunately, he met with a motorcycle accident in his mid-forties that left him with long-term memory challenges. For an interim period, I succeeded him while a replacement was found. Sadly, he did prepare me to take over for him.

Next up is Steve Atkins who hired me into his organization United Family Life, a Fortis company in the pre-need insurance industry. He was an accountant, studious and soft spoken. Steve loved humor and always sought to lighten the mood by recounting one anecdote or another. He'd finish with the statement, "I'm full of useless information." The things he said were never useless. He taught life lessons through storytelling and self-directed humor. He led by coaching. I remember my first employee review where he explained I had done really well. He summed up the year and set the tone going forward by saying with a smile, "The reward for really great work is even more hard work." Then, he gave me more challenges, and my career propelled forward. Ultimately, Steve coached me into leadership and growth in the organization.

Photo 4-6: Another one of my career influencers, Grover Thomas

Another strong mentor in the same pre-need company was Grover Thomas, its CEO. During his tenure, I had the privilege of working on the team that built the company's diversity strategy to emerge from a time when African Americans were historically underrepresented in leadership roles and absent from senior leadership. In addition, I was a charter member of Project Mentoring, a team that designed and developed a mentoring program for promising African American leaders. Our team's objectives were to prepare the members for leadership roles, support each other as we pursued career objectives and build a program that was sustainable as our company evolved. Mentoring with Grover was an exhilarating experience.

He'd risen through the ranks in his career through a combination of will, skill, determination, calculated risk-taking and right-time, right-place execution. Grover taught me to never limit myself and to know my value. He also counseled me not to allow a job or role to limit me or my growth. He said, "A company will never pay you what you're worth; they will pay you what you're worth to them." He showed me how to increase my earning capacity. I took his advice, determining to never be limited by what existed, but what I could help create. I once told Grover, "I am only limited by experience and exposure. Given the opportunity, I will make the difference."

Photo 4-7: My best friend Paula E. Bonds

The last mentor I want to highlight is my best friend Paula E. Bonds, J.D., LL.M, a practicing civil rights, corporate and family law attorney. Our friendship lasted 25 plus years. Paula always challenged me ethically, intellectually, morally and socially to expand my thinking. We shared countless mutual mentoring moments. A favorite response of hers, whenever my assessment leaned too heavily on what others could or should do, was, "Sandra, we're not working on them right now." Our long friendship was cut short when she passed away in July 2017, leaving a quarter century of wisdom, inspiration and legacy through her personal journals.

"Silence can be misinterpreted. I've resolved instead to add my voice to the conversation and to be authentic with my views." – Sandra Broughton

---

While I've enjoyed positive lessons from my mentors, there were also two lessons I have learned not to emulate:

1. **When confronted with high risk initiatives, do not rush forward when initiating a high risk strategy.** Instead, take time to educate and involve others. Avoid future opposition and possible derailment by ensuring stakeholder engagement early and removing barriers to success.

2. **Silence buys nothing.** Having been mentored by both men and women, I found that women were less prone to encourage speaking up. Women have cautioned me to be careful, not to take the risk or to stay within perceived boundaries. I have been coached to say nothing

or pick my battles. Over time and through experience, I've learned that silence can be misinterpreted. I've resolved instead to add my voice to the conversation and to be authentic with my views. I believe women at large are making progress in this area.

My letter to my mentors would express gratitude that words cannot easily describe. I would share my story as written here and then tell them:

I have concluded that we are all the sum of our exposure and experiences. Thank you for helping to shape who I am and what I will become. Your influence in my life cannot be measured. Because of you, I've had the opportunity to contribute to so wonderful a book. You get the credit because it's your story that I am telling. I realize I've had the blessing of many mentors. You were among the best.

With love and appreciation,
Sandra

The Director, Customer Experience for Southern Company Gas, Sandra Broughton has also served as an active CS Week Planning Committee member. She recently helped lead the implementation of Southern Company Gas' replacement customer information system. Headquartered in Atlanta, GA, Southern Company Gas is the largest natural gas-only distribution company in the United States. Its 5,000 employees proudly serve 4.5 million utility customers.

CHAPTER 5

LISA CAGNOLATTI
Vice President of Customer Service Operations (Retired)
Southern California Edison

Photo 5-1: Lisa Cagnolatti

I always knew my mother was a good role model, but now I realize she was also a prophet; some might even call her a fortune teller. Jeri Cagnolatti was the kind of woman whom I respected and looked up to. She was strong, independent and full of wisdom and sage sayings like this one: "Never date the men you work with, Lisa. Always consider them to be your colleagues and not your potential dates." In hindsight, I've come to understand what my mother knew first-hand. As an x-ray technician and officer manager who worked for doctors, my mother had seen and heard a lot of shenanigans between men and women, between bosses and employees, between professionals and staff. Her advice seems especially prescient in our current culture stained by harassment, coarseness and corruption. When faced with ethical dilemmas, when others' actions and language are inappropriate but unchecked, and when hard situations unmask stark differences between my moral compass and others' north needles, I will always be true to myself.

Photo 5-2: My mother, Jeri Cagnolatti

A firebrand compared to my more introverted father, Jeri was a practical person and strongly driven to be financially upwardly mobile. She taught me to have a strategic relationship with money so that it worked for me, not vice versa. She stressed the importance of living below my means as a way of creating headroom in the budget to invest. Note to self: she used the word, "invest" not "save," because investing would allow me to be actively involved in making my money work for me. My husband and I adopted her philosophy about investing, setting firm five-year net worth goals that we exceeded each time. Here I am in February 2018, able to retire at age 56 after a 34-year professional career. We are set to relocate to Arizona for its lower cost of living and to be closer to my brother and sister. And I can proudly announce that the torch has been passed on to the next generation. My older son, just 27 years young, recently bought his first investment property. My mother's lessons live on!

"'Growth only happens,' she taught, 'when you push yourself outside your comfort zone.'" – Lisa Cagnolatti

---

When I started my first professional position as a Team Manager at Procter & Gamble's manufacturing plant in Oxnard, California, Sue Hockenmaier was my boss, and she became an important mentor for me. Sue was the first to teach me lessons of self-awareness about my behavior, image and interpersonal interactions. It was the early 1980s, and we were just starting to learn about a company's responsibility to prevent sexual harassment in the workplace. Talking together one day, I asked Sue jokingly, "I'm not *unattractive*… why does no one ever harass me?" Her answer opened the door of self-awareness. She said with a smile, "Honey, you have a chip on your shoulder the size of Texas. No one is ever going to harass you." I was not aware that I was giving off a "tough girl" vibe. It was very instructive feedback, and I took her words to heart.

I stayed for two years at P&G, and when they offered me a promotion, the positions were in faraway American cities. I instead chose to make a career change and take a position at the Southern California Gas Company. There, I met Carolyn Green, the Environmental Affairs Manager at the time. She reached out to me in my early days as an Account Executive in the Commercial/Industrial Customer Division. During our mentoring sessions,

Photo 5-3: Carolyn Green, my early mentor at Southern California Gas Company

Carolyn told me a couple things that stuck, and I've paid them forward with my mentees. The first piece of advice certainly made an impact on me – an ambitious woman in her mid-twenties: never let the grass grow under your feet. She said, "If you've been in a job longer than three years, you have passed your expiration date and should move on." Carolyn didn't necessarily mean leave the company; rather, she encouraged me to challenge myself to learn something different every few years to accelerate my professional development. "Growth only happens," she taught, "when you push yourself outside your comfort zone."

> "Never forget, you are always on stage as a leader, and everything you do and everything you say matters."
> – Lisa Cagnolatti

Carolyn and I also discussed the difference in corporate cultures between Procter & Gamble and the Gas Company. P&G had an open and nimble culture, a workplace where anyone could walk into the plant manager's office to talk, and everyone was part of the team. The Gas Company, like many utility companies, was quite the opposite: slow to change, risk averse and hierarchical. Carolyn continued, "Sometimes in your career you will encounter 'rampant mediocrity' because people often find themselves in positions that don't challenge them very much. They get complacent; they do the bare minimum." She went on, "Do not succumb to the mediocrity. Remember that you are a high achiever. Your work ethic is excellent. Don't forget who you are, no matter where you land. Behave like a superstar no matter your work assignment or the environment you find yourself in because that's who you are."

Those words have guided me through many challenges throughout my career. Sometimes I'd find myself in departments with bosses that I could look up to, sometimes not so much. Even now, in my last weeks of work before my retirement date at the end of February, my colleagues and staff comment about my 'Energizer Bunny' work ethic. They comment about my punctuality and preparation for meetings, surprised that I'm still engaged and passionate about the work that I'll be leaving to others very shortly. I answer, "I don't know any other way to be." Carolyn's observations and encouragement

Photo 5-4: Dick Rosenblum, my sounding board at Southern California Edison

gave me the confidence to be me. Though she left Southern California Gas to become an air quality official in southern California and then Vice President of Health, Environment and Safety for Sunoco Oil Company and ultimately a successful entrepreneur, Carolyn's affirmation of me, my values, ethics and ambitions are engraved into my memory and into my heart.

The next two professional mentors taught me more lessons about how I represented myself to others and why it mattered. The first was Dick Rosenblum, Senior Vice President of Transmission and Distribution at Southern California Edison. When I was a Region Manager in Edison's Construction/Maintenance Department, Dick was my sounding board. He told me two things that stuck. Number one: never forget you are always on stage as a leader, and everything you do and everything you say matters. His second lesson had to do with ethics and integrity. Though I didn't understand at the time that those virtues were capable of

---

"'No matter how people behave or treat you, you never let it change who you are.'" – Lisa Cagnolatti

---

sealing a competitive advantage, Dick set the example. During this time, he was dealing with personnel situations where people were telling and sending inappropriate jokes. This behavior, according to Dick's moral compass, was unacceptable, and he held his leaders accountable, including me to report all incidents that we became aware of. He expected us to be stewards of the culture and hold ourselves and others to high standards. If identified, Dick expected us to raise up complaints to Human Resources and work cooperatively with them to eradicate inappropriate behavior from the work environment.

The second was Stephen Xavier, my executive coach when I first became an executive at Edison in 2004. Stephen said, "No matter how people behave or treat you, you never let it change who you are." That advice sure came in handy when I later faced a boss whose behavior troubled me. Frankly, this boss and I saw the world very differently. I felt that he didn't value me or my style, and I didn't value his. I personally witnessed him engage in behavior that did not mesh with my values. Even though he was called out for his style and behaviors, he persisted. Stephen's words gave me courage and the confidence to stand for my principles and personal integrity through those challenging times.

These mentors, starting with my mother through various professional mentors, and the lessons they taught, remain with me today. Though my mom and dad have both passed, I am blessed that Sue and Carolyn and Dick and Stephen are still around. Occasionally, I think of them fondly, and if I were to ever speak with them again, here is what I would say: "Thank you so much for caring enough to share your wisdom with me. Your advice and counsel helped me accelerate my growth and reach my potential. Most importantly, you created in me a leader who has been able to help develop other leaders throughout my career. Without your trust in me, your guidance through tough times and your sage advice, I would not have achieved this level of success in all aspects of my life. Thank you."

Retired in early 2018, Lisa Cagnolatti was the vice president of customer service operations for Southern California Edison. As one of the nation's largest electric utilities, So Cal Edison delivers power to 15 million people in a 50,000 square-miles service territory across central, coastal and Southern California, excluding the City of Los Angeles and some other cities. Making a difference in education, the environment, public safety and preparedness and civic engagement, its parent company Edison International gave $21.8 million to community programs in 2017.

CHAPTER 6

EILEEN CAMPBELL
Vice President Customer Service
Alectra Utilities

Photo 6-1: Eileen Campbell

Growing up and to this day, it was my businessman dad Albert Campbell who influences how I conduct myself in business and my personal life. He instilled in my two siblings and me the importance of working hard, working smart and treating everyone with respect. My dad didn't like it when I casually said one day that the man who delivered milk to our house "was just a milkman." I can still hear the lecture about how everyone has an important role to play as part of the team, and the milkman was the face of the company to the customer — a very important role! I took that lesson to heart. My dad had a charismatic manner that drew people to him (maybe it was his warm smile or perhaps his Irish accent). He prided himself on knowing his employees' names and those of their children, and I have

"Business and personal success were built and strengthened through the power of relationships and the value of everyone's contributions." – Eileen Campbell

Photo 6-2: My dad Albert Campbell and me

followed his lead on this front. The primary lesson for me was that my dad's business and personal success were built and strengthened through the power of relationships and the value of everyone's contributions. Those are key factors that I consider as part of my success. My dad is gone now, but his voice still echoes in my head. I try to hold myself to the same standards that he did. To me and others, he was an important mentor and inspiration.

Don't distance yourself from the front line.
– Eileen Campbell

My utility career started straight out of high school in the billing department answering customer inquiries both on the telephone and at the front counter. Some might say my formal business education started as hands-on learning. It wasn't until years later that I pursued supporting diploma programs at college and university. I was fortunate in the early years to have a mentor in Errol McCluskey, the billing department manager who recognized my potential. As one of three female candidates, I joined an in-house manager-in-training program. For a very conservative-minded utility in the early 1980s, it was quite a revelation to promote talent from within – especially a woman. Because I was a young management trainee in a male-dominated environment, Errol encouraged me to believe in myself. He was well-intended when he suggested that I should distance myself from frontline staff and not smile so much. I didn't follow this advice though. One of the highest compliments that I ever received was from a frontline staff person who said, "When you are with the team, everyone knows you are the boss, but you still fit in." To me, this is a big part of my leadership style that has brought success.

Max Cananzi, President of Alectra Utilities, has by far been the greatest influencer of my career development. He has a proven track record of surrounding himself with great people and promoting from within the organization. To be clear, Max can be challenging and demanding. With Max, this comes from being well informed, industry-connected, and it seems he

Photo 6-3: Max Cananzi, one of my greatest career influencers

is always one step ahead all the time. He taught me the importance of solid decision-making based on facts and a little gut feel. When Max promoted me to Vice-President of Customer Service in 2006, I wasn't fully confident that I was ready for the job, but he said, "Time to jump in, and I will help you." And he did. Following his lead of being known and visible within the business sector, I have taken on greater leadership roles outside our utility. He shared his experience that knowing what went on inside the walls of our business was not enough. Max suggested that following current trends in other businesses and understanding the competitive landscape was critical to my success. And he was right. Networking and building relationships with other business leaders have helped me to grow and evolve with the ever-changing business climate. I am very fortunate to work for a boss like Max. He taught me that a good boss manages outcomes and inspires the team to do their best. He also taught me that my actions speak louder than words because how I react to situations and my behaviours affect everyone around me. It's game on every day!

> ## Take on greater leadership roles outside your job.
> ## – Eileen Campbell

Over the past thirty-seven years, I've had my share of supervisors; most I count as my mentors. Often, they weren't even aware of this role, but I carefully observed their business and interpersonal interactions. Each had unique ways of motivating or demotivating people with their behaviours. One supervisor would walk around the office with a stern expression, and the employees would scatter. He managed the office by fear, and he told me that when I walked by and people stopped talking, it was a sign of respect, and I should be proud of this accomplishment. My supervisor meant well; however, my leadership style has instead focused on fostering an environment that was supportive, open and transparent to achieve an engaged workforce.

To the many mentors who encouraged me through the years, I send my heartfelt thanks. So simply put, these few words may seem insignificant, but those identified here, and unnamed others have unselfishly invested time and passion to help me along my path. From the early years of being a customer service representative, then as part of the manager-in-training program and then to my promotion as Vice President Customer Service,

I've never taken the opportunities presented to me for granted. I've experienced amalgamation with neighbouring cities/towns and mergers that have seen our company's boundaries expand and reach over a million customers. Being successful takes perseverance and determination. I've learned that no personal growth comes from taking the easy road. For these lessons taught and learned, I thank my mentors who have influenced my business and personal life. I've never thought of my work as just a job, but rather a career that is also my passion.

Alectra's family of energy companies distributes electricity to nearly one million customers in Ontario's Greater Golden Horseshoe Area and provides innovative energy solutions to these and thousands more across Ontario. The Alectra family of companies includes Alectra Inc., Alectra Utilities Corporation and Alectra Energy Solutions. Eileen Campbell is Alectra Utilities' Vice President, Customer Service.

CHAPTER 7

CHRIS CARDENAS
Customer Services Vice President
PPL Electric Utilities

Photo 7-1: Chris Cardenas

Valuing and appreciating others, regardless of the job they perform, was a lesson I learned from my father while he worked three jobs to support our family. Domingo T. Cardenas grew up on the streets of San Antonio, Texas, with many siblings and few options for people with high school diplomas. The US Marine Corps offered him a ticket out and up from the barrio, and for 20 years he served honorably and achieved the rank of staff sergeant during the Vietnam war era. My father had an incredible work ethic. His quality of work was consistently meticulous. He was my primary mentor during my formative years, teaching me the importance of a solid work ethic, respect for others, working hard and delivering a quality product in everything I do.

To supplement his military pay, my father worked side jobs, taking me along so we could spend time together. While he emptied trash cans and performed other part-time work, he taught me valuable life lessons which I've held on to throughout my career. Our associates on the front line, whether wearing hardhats or headsets, have the toughest jobs. Their ability to consistently deliver on increasingly demanding job expectations and still serve our customers with respect and kindness is what sets them apart. I'm reminded daily how important their jobs are and how blessed I am to work with people who are so dedicated. I value and respect who they are and what they do every day. It's just the way my father taught me to treat others, and I make sure my children use the same epithets.

Value and appreciate others regardless of the job they perform. – Chris Cardenas

---

In one of my first leadership roles, I worked for Diane Roberts, then Senior Director of Customer Service Operations at Nextel for about five years. She taught me the significance of authenticity and the importance of being an authentic leader. Performance excellence, operational effectiveness and the ability to navigate political waters were parts of the ongoing lesson plan in her informal classroom. In one of our first heated debates, she exclaimed, "Chris, just shut up and listen." Though I was adamant about not getting wrapped up in work politics, Diane laid out how important it was to navigate the waters and to understand why knowing and playing the political game is critical. She explained that it wasn't about sacrificing my core values; rather, it was about acknowledging innate human tendencies towards power and control. Recognizing and adapting to people with ulterior motives is an essential leadership skillset. She continued, "There are leaders who view their authority as a divine right and others who view their leadership role as a privilege. The former are the same people who compromise relationships and corrupt trust." Diane helped me learn how to confidently perform and navigate at all levels of the business. I learned how to balance my innate ability to build relationships and engender trust while simultaneously keeping my eyes wide-open for those leadership styles vastly different than my own. She explained, "Once your team understands your core values and trusts you have their best interest at heart, they'll follow anywhere and do anything for you."

Her lessons crystalized for me at US Cellular where I was hired to lead a tele-sales team. Sales is indeed a different animal, and I found myself in uncharted waters. Sales quotas and daily performance pressures made the new environment particularly stressful. Diane's wise words prepared me for the challenge. I worked to get to know my staff and was able to leverage those relationships to form a team dynamic marked by trust and respect. Exceeding quotas thereafter came easy for our team because they wanted to prove me a good leader and never wanted to let me down. I applied Diane's principles consistently, and they work for me every time. I fill my executive toolbelt with these values today.

Be an authentic leader. – Chris Cardenas

Like many, I've learned more from bad leaders than from good ones. Carrying my father's and Diane's lessons with me, I learned early on to never neglect the frontline workers who do the heavy lifting, whether face-to-face, in the field or in the contact centers. Together, my team and I create a sense of family and a goal-oriented community, one in which everyone is valued and an important part of the whole. When you've worn the headset or strapped on a tool belt, it is easier to relate to the needs of the frontline associates. You never forget the dynamic of customer interactions, both negative and positive, which serves you well when you're an executive considering changes in structure, people and processes. I like to know how my team is feeling, and we trust each other because I've been there too. From legacy processes, to documentation, to service offerings and resolving customer issues; field and customer service representatives have a lot to remember to be successful with a single interaction. Their jobs require emotional maturity, resilience and confidence to de-escalate heightened conversations. Our reps are masters at their craft. It becomes second nature to them, and I applaud their abilities and attitudes to remain positive, to not take things personally and to take pride in doing their jobs well. Their feelings of accomplishment are important to me. Valuing our associates translates into valuing customers and together that helps us engage more effectively and enhance our customer experience.

"'Once your team understands your core values and trusts you have their best interest at heart, they'll follow anywhere and do anything for you.'" – Chris Cardenas

---

To my two named mentors, Domingo T. Cardenas and Diane Roberts, thank you for keeping me grounded and showing me the value of being an authentic leader. As a native Texan, I cut my teeth on many of its favorite sayings like, "Sometimes it's okay to lie, cheat and steal, but you can never be disrespectful." I was raised on Southern hospitality, and those lessons are deeply engrained. Because I believe leadership is a privilege and not a divine right, being an authentic leader defines my personal style and approach. What you see is what you get. That includes lapsing into other

Texas expressions like "y'all", "fixin'-to" and "fire" (pronounced with one syllable). My foundation instilled by my father made me who I am, and Diane encouraged values of caring about people, building relationships, managing to the individual not the team and loving the people with whom I work. After all, we spend more time with co-workers than we do with our families, and we are all here for the same reason, a job and the paycheck. So, let's have fun while we're working together, supporting and respecting each other along the way. I believe effective leadership produces happy associates and happy associates treat customers well. This circular relationship repeats itself every day in innumerable and unmeasurable ways.

Headquartered in Allentown, PA, PPL Electric Utilities has been an industry leader for nearly 30 years by offering programs that spend more than $70 million annually helping low-income customers pay heating bills. PPL is also the first electric utility in Pennsylvania to track hourly usage for all its customers via an advanced metering system. Using the power of that information, they are developing ways to give their 1.4 million customers new options, tips and energy use advice. Chris Cardenas is PPL Electric Utilities' Customer Services Vice President.

CHAPTER 8

ELLIS CHANDLEE

Director of Commercial and Corporate Applications (Retired)

ONE Gas

Photo 8-1: Ellis Chandlee

I was very fortunate to have my father as my earliest mentor. It seems too common these days that children do not get to have the benefit of a two-parent household. I was also very fortunate that my father was a patient man. He spent the time to pass on hard-fought lessons he learned. His main lessons were around having a solid work ethic and always doing a good job. His catch-phrase was, "A job worth doing... is worth doing well!" When I was cutting the family yard, it was hard for me to appreciate those words. Cutting the grass in Oklahoma on summer days in 100-degree heat is something you want done quickly with little worry about perfection. My father would point out things that could have been done better. Then, he would ask me, "Do you want to find your own mistakes, or do you want someone else to point them out? Better yet, do it right the first time and no worries!"

"'A job worth doing… is worth doing well!'" – Ellis Chandlee

My dad's words and attitude reflect values I later drilled into my three kids. My oldest daughter is a successful engineer. The twins are starting college next week, with my son headed into engineering and my daughter into nursing. Throughout their formative years, I shared the wisdom and mentoring my father shared with me.

"Understanding the underlying business issue allowed me to construct a better mousetrap." – Ellis Chandlee

---

Louise Jones was my business counterpart when I started at Oklahoma Natural Gas (a division of ONE Gas, formerly ONEOK, Inc.). She was a very determined individual who rose up from the ranks. Her first job at the company was as a secretary in a small remote office. She retired as a Director with over 60 years of service. Being from an IT background, it is sometimes difficult for me to fully understand the needs of the business. Louise helped me think like a person in the business and not just an IT guy who typically likes to solve problems in a logical way but doesn't often think outside of the box. I learned that simply creating something to satisfy a stated requirement does not allow for the best solution. Louise taught me that understanding the underlying business issue allowed me to construct a better mousetrap.

But to be able to think like a person in the business, I had to know the business and their issues like how they make their rate of return and what challenges they face. Together, Louise and I developed several incredible solutions for ONEOK/ONE Gas. This manner of thinking carried on past her retirement, and it has allowed me and my IT colleagues to have a mind-set around business solutions that set our team apart from our peers.

I once had a boss during my career that was all 'stick' and no 'carrot.' From him, I learned that fear and intimidation only work on certain people and only for so long. People need to know how they can be rewarded for their performance. The 'stick' method makes people perform their jobs out of fear and cannot be sustained. Sometimes a reward as small and simple as a compliment or acknowledgement goes a long way. I have found it is always better to have employees who are self-motivated.

I was fortunate that I was able to tell my father shortly before his passing how much he impacted my life. No child wants to admit that their parents are right, but at least I was able to tell him that he was ALWAYS RIGHT. He just looked at me in his weakened condition and said, "It took you long enough!" and then he winked at me. It took me a long time to appreciate his advice and warnings. If I could write to him, I would tell him how his lessons and advice were invested wisely. Those same words of wisdom were passed down to his grandchildren. It did not always make me the most favorite dad at the time. I could see the same 'blah blah blah' look in their eyes that I probably gave my father. Luckily, my twins have their older sister to tell them that they may not appreciate my advice and my way of running things, but they may one day own a different perspective, like I did with my father. Thank you, Pop!

Don't be all stick and no carrot. – Ellis Chandlee

I ran into Ms. Jones recently. I was able to express my appreciation to her. I told her that she made me a better employee by seeing things from the perspective of the business. If I were able to send her a letter, I would tell her that people of her caliber are rare these days. Not only was she able to instill great business sense in me, but she was a great employee to emulate. Understanding the business has made me a better employee for ONE Gas. My team also has been able to create some valuable functionality for our company's customers and users along the way.

Photo 8-2: Me, retired and relaxed by the pool

If I could write to the individual who managed by 'stick,' I'd tell him his methodology might have had its place at one time, but that is ancient history. Using fear and intimidation does not work well anymore (if it ever did). Especially today, with the influx of millennials into the workforce, this tactic would fall way short of its goal. Today's college graduates have different motivations and expectations than previous generations, like setting people up to succeed by giving them realistic goals and following through by matching performance with rewards.

Comprised of three companies in Oklahoma, Kansas and Texas, ONE Gas's 3,000 employees serve over 2 million customers is one of America's largest natural gas utilities. A 100 percent regulated utility, ONE Gas's history closely tracks the exploration and expansion of Oklahoma. Headquartered in Tulsa, OK, ONE Gas has five corporate pillars: safety, inclusion and diversity, ethics, service and value. Ellis Chandlee was its Director of Commercial and Corporate Applications. Before his recent retirement, Chandlee had been involved in significant technology changes that supported business functions and contributed to a satisfying customer experience.

CHAPTER 9

CHIMAOBI CHIJIOKE
Director of Customer Care
BGE, an Exelon Company

Photo 9-1: Chimaobi Chijioke

My name is Chimaobi. It's a Nigerian name that means, "God knows your heart." I am grateful to my parents for giving me such an auspicious name, and I believe it's my legacy to extend its meaning through my relationships, particularly those in my workplace, Baltimore Gas and Electric. Leadership in most instances is an art observed and passed down from mentors to their mentees. In my case, I have had the opportunity of being led by inspirational leaders who lit a fire in me to chart a distinctive path of defining what it takes to be a good leader.

My leadership lessons date back to my first days as a supervisor. In that first team meeting, my Associate Director acknowledged and encouraged everyone at the meeting to give an opinion or feedback on the topics of discussion. Then, she took the time to appreciate and support any idea that

"'Correction makes you better; it is not meant to be punitive.'" – Chimaobi Chijioke

was raised regardless of its value. Because of that encouragement, members took the time to prepare and go the extra mile to provide an idea, engage in the dialogue or offer an opinion. When I pointed out this tactic to her and asked why she went the extra mile to do this, she responded, "Chima, most leaders will tell you, 'You can force a horse to the river, but you cannot force it to drink. Our job as leaders is not to force horses to drink water but to make them want to drink it.'"

"'A leader needs to be confident and calm for your team.'" – Chimaobi Chijioke

---

About 10 years ago while employed at Verizon Wireless, I was privileged to work with Connie Chaffins, then Associate Director for Customer Service. Connie taught me what it meant to be a leader by caring for people and teaching them how to be successful. Through a combination of words and actions, she developed the knack of making others feel comfortable even when offering correction. She understood the opportunities that correction offered and would say, "Correction makes you better; it is not meant to be punitive." I worked with Connie for about a year and a half, but her lessons have remained with me since. Even today, I can pick up the phone and call her when I need a listening ear for guidance.

Photo 9-2: Morlon Bell-Izzard, a key mentor

Another mentor who offered important business lessons was Morlon Bell-Izzard. Her lesson was about being calm under pressure regardless of the situation. "There's always a solution," she would say, "and a leader needs to be confident and calm for your team." When BGE rolled out its new customer care and billing system a couple years ago, everything seemed to be going wrong. I called Morlon and her reaction matched her lesson. After listening to my agitated explanation, she responded, "It can't get any worse, and your team is looking to you to engender confidence. Don't dwell on the details of the problems. Instead, focus on solutions." These reassurances buoyed my spirits and gave me the confidence to work through the issues. I had observed her calm, positive demeanor in the past, and it gave me the confidence to work through the issues and wear a can-do attitude.

Morlon's mentoring lesson was completely challenged by another director I worked for who felt the best way to drive performance was to punish those who didn't meet goals. Her methods alienated staff and outcomes declined. To counteract that well-intentioned but punitive directive, I chose to figure out opportunities to help my staff succeed. My heart led me to follow a positive approach, encouraging my staff to understand the rationale behind decisions, policies and procedures so that they wanted to follow them.

To mentors who have impacted me immensely, my letters of appreciation would be short and direct:

"Dear Connie, 'You started this.'"

"Dear Morlon, 'I'm trying to make you proud of me.'"

"Don't dwell on the details of the problems. Instead, focus on solutions." – Chimaobi Chijioke

---

After many years in leadership roles, I know myself. I must lead with a grateful, giving and loving heart. By sowing seeds of calmness, confidence and positive opportunities in individuals, I, in turn, create a desire for them to want to grow. With and through others, I continue to reap a bountiful harvest because God knows my heart.

Chimaobi Chijioke is the Director of Customer Care for Baltimore Gas and Electric, Maryland's largest natural gas and electric utility that delivers power to more than 1.25 million electric customers and more than 650,000 natural gas customers. A subsidiary of Exelon Corporation, BGE has a 200-plus year history of serving Central Maryland. Its past and present story is grounded in integrity, forward thinking, openness to ideas and principled decision-making, values that are intrinsic to daily customer service operations.

CHAPTER 10

KATY COOK
Director Transformation - CIS Strategy
Liberty Utilities

Photo 10-1: Katy Cook

It sounds hokey, but my childhood mentor was my older sister Alison Morgan. That poor kid had to look after me from a young age, and I was pretty undisciplined. She was the responsible older sister who had to get me to school on time, pick me up after school and ride public transit with me. She taught me some valuable life lessons – be on time, don't run away when you are angry, and take the time to refuel.

If you are not on time you miss the bus, and everyone on the bus will move ahead without you. If you run away you will get lost, and you can't be cheered up if you can't be found and a lot of people will worry about you. After a hard day, a small piece of chocolate can clear and refresh the mind. These life lessons apply today in business as much as they did to a rebellious kid. Being on time shows respect and commitment. Running away is rarely productive; rather, talking through issues, gaining perspective and working to support each other builds strong teams. And after a hard day, do something that energizes your spirit.

Photo 10-2: Afshan Kinder, my mentor at Sprint Canada

Afshan Kinder is an incredible person. I first met Afshan at Sprint Canada, where she was Director of Customer Service for Residential Services, and I reported to her. The first thing I noticed about Afshan was her size. She's petite, and then, almost simultaneously, I felt her strength. She would walk into a room composed, confident and prepared. Afshan taught me to be accountable, to have integrity and to respect others. Now, I had some of these qualities already, but what Afshan did was demonstrate these qualities very clearly, and as a result, she allowed her whole team to grow and learn from her behaviour. The most visible sign of Afshan's accountability was something she would do for our customers. At the bottom of every invoice her name and title were printed. If there was an issue, and sometimes there was, customers would call and ask to speak to him. She never refused a call. No, this is not a typo. Customers regularly assumed Afshan was a man, and she took it in stride. By speaking to customers, she understood what was working well, what our issues were and most importantly, what our customer expectations were. She did not randomly assign credits to the customer account in question or dismiss the customer service representative that had dealt with the customer. She held firm to the policies and practices the company had put in place. She offered fair solutions that demonstrated the company's care while maintaining the integrity of the business. After these conversations, she circled back to the managers and supervisors and provided near real-time feedback on her experience. She also used her knowledge to influence the senior teams to address issues and prioritize change. I kept in touch with Afshan as she and her business partners built their consulting business, SwitchGear. Whenever I reached out, her response time was still impeccable and her strength still palpable.

> "Be on time, don't run away when you are angry, and take the time to refuel." – Katy Cook

Other mentors have not been so positive or modeled such admirable behaviours. I recall being caught off guard the first time I presented in front of a former boss. He gave me feedback right after the presentation on how to improve. Because it had been years since I was given such specific and constructive feedback, I actually appreciated it. His points were spot on; for example, I had started the presentation strong but was not a great closer because I lost momentum. His lesson was powerful. However, he

Give honest, direct feedback privately and as near-time as possible. – Katy Cook

had another tendency that was much less desirable – passive aggression. He would sabotage my work publicly, asking for updates on projects that were never prioritized or agreed to. He would complement work and then add "but" to the end of his statement, making me question if I was successful or not. His sarcasm was subtle. As a result, I spent years wondering if I was fantastic or just a few steps from being walked out the door.

Sometimes the best lessons learned are the ones you do not emulate. As a rule, I try to give honest, direct feedback privately and as near real-time as possible. I validate the scope and priorities with team members before we present to larger groups. When I compliment work, I am specific and precise with my words, and there is rarely a "but." Recognizing the passive aggressive behaviour in others helped me see it in myself. I've changed how I interact with team members. People know where they stand, and I have toned down the sarcasm a lot.

Photo 10-3: Me and Alison ride for Heart and Stroke

If I were writing to any of the people I have written about here, I would say thank you. Thank you, Alison for always pushing me to keep up, for not letting me get lost and for sharing your time with me to refuel. You continue to inspire me, and I am thankful for every moment we spend together, particularly on the road, on our bikes, refueling.

I would thank Afshan for demonstrating accountability. In the twenty years I have been working, I have never seen a leader so willing to put his or her name in print and to stand behind the company. The human connection,

"When I compliment work, I am specific and precise with my words, and there is rarely a 'but.'" – Katy Cook

the integrity and the respect it demonstrates to others continues to be a best practice. Every time I receive an invoice, a marketing offer or a letter I look for a signature, some form of commitment from someone proud enough of their company to stand behind it. Those leaders truly represent service excellence.

To my former boss who offered constructive criticism intermingled with passive aggressive sarcasm, I would also extend my appreciation. Because I am deeply committed to my work and have broad shoulders, I was able to internalize and learn from those public criticisms leveled against me. Ensuring the company's success and being a productive part of that effort remain my highest goals. In my interactions, I publicly encourage others to share my passion for sincerity, service excellence and honesty. A lesson delivered on the down-low years ago became an opportunity for me to take the high road now and in the future.

Katy Cook is the Director Transformation – CIS Strategy for Liberty Utilities, a high growth company that owns and operates regulated water, wastewater, natural gas and electric utilities across small and mid-sized US communities in 12 states. Liberty's service delivery to its 750,000-plus customers is characterized by local community support, compliance with environmental regulations and safe, reliable utility services.

CHAPTER 11

SUE DAULTON
Senior Management Analyst
Tacoma Public Utilities

Photo 11-1: Sue Daulton

Mark Twain, one of America's most beloved authors, is credited with a saying that embodies my life and career mentors, from earliest childhood to my career today: "Action speaks louder than words but not nearly as often." Starting with my parents, Mary and Hiram Olsen, I learned early about their sense of commitment to our community by their life-long example. Participation on boards and volunteering with church, school and community groups was part of their weekly schedule. They demonstrated their belief that each of us can make a difference. Their example, in turn, inspired my personal commitment to volunteering. Tacoma Public Utilities has established a wonderful structure that supports and empowers employees to participate in a variety of ways that strengthen the communities we serve. I have also been fortunate to serve on several local and national boards and participate in moving forward their missions which has enriched my personal and professional life. From industry organizations created to support users and advance system functionality like ASUG to my tenure with CS Week, its

> "'Action speaks louder than words but not nearly as often.'"
> – Sue Daulton

Planning Committee and Board of Directors, volunteering has been foundational to my personal growth. By working, collaborating and leading others, apart from my work responsibilities at TPU, I've gained access and exposure to utility leaders and learned many lessons from them.

I have been lucky to have had some wonderful mentors from my first job as a summer intern through the present. As a summer intern in an economic development group, I was attending a meeting where the CEO asked me what I thought about the subject being discussed. He said everyone adds value to the conversation. That sense of inclusion has guided and informed me over my career.

Photo 11-2: Steve Hatcher, Tacoma Public Utilities' Customer Service Director

Another mentor Steve Hatcher, the Utilities' Customer Services Director, introduced me over a dozen years ago to the concept of cross-organizational teams. He helped me understand the value of forming teams with the right composition of skills and diversity of ideas. My early impressions of collaboration and active participation as a team member were further developed with Steve's mentoring tip: build strong teams to develop common goals and organizational support for strategic initiatives. His lesson has borne fruit many times, including when we evaluated changing our billing cycles from bimonthly to monthly; when we investigated and changed due dates to give customers more time to pay their bills; and when we redesigned our website. By expanding our horizons beyond "who in customer service should be a team member," we broadened the base to include, for example, someone from legal, a resource from communications and marketing, analytics specialists and operational subject matter experts depending on our goals and scope. We reached out to include resources across the organization, not just those in customer service. Customer and stakeholder involvement has been significant. Because of this inclusiveness, we have been able to limit unintended consequences that someone else had to live with before we employed this resource model. We've expanded our scope into a broader, organizational view. Besides understanding what creates great teams, Steve also has a great sense of humor, and he's passionate about serving customers.

Value volunteerism. – Sue Daulton

Over the years, I've occasionally been offered advice from those whose timing or message I've had to ignore. A few minutes before making my first presentation to our Board, I was approached by a manager who wanted to relay a series of prior painful experiences he had while presenting to this Board. This information wasn't helpful and had me beginning to dread a wonderful experience for a young manager. I jumped in and presented what would become the first of many presentations over my career. Because I really understood the topic and felt confident that what we were asking the Board to support was right, I was able to set aside this negative lesson just minutes before. So, what did I learn? Since then, I actively try to help people who are making major presentations get ready in advance. We review the presentation and practice weeks ahead, with me pointing out things to emphasize and consider, both in delivery and content. By helping others be prepared and knowledgeable and not be afraid or nervous about presenting, I counteract the ill-timed advice that could have derailed me.

Develop cross-organizational teams. – Sue Daulton

If I could write a letter to some of my mentors today, I wouldn't. Being a hugger, I would instead give big hugs to both my mom and dad and thank them for all the life lessons, encouragement and love they so generously gave me. That would say without words what's important to me.

Photo 11-3: Mary and Hiram Olsen, my parents

Municipally-owned, Tacoma Public Utilities is the largest city department and is governed by the Tacoma Public Utility Board. Its 1,350 employees provide services to 176,000 electric customers, 24,000 cable customers, nearly 100,000 water customers and the Port of Tacoma and surrounding customers for railroad freight switching. Besides her role as Senior Management Analyst at TPU, Sue Daulton also serves on the CS Week Board of Directors and Planning Committee and is a utility community facilitator for ASUG - Americas' SAP Users' Group.

CHAPTER 12

FRED DAUM
Director of Customer Contact and Billing
PSEG Long Island

Photo 12-1: Fred Daum

I took my seat as always in anticipation of class starting. Soon the teacher would be coming through the door with today's lesson. The great thing about this class was that you never really knew what the lesson of the day would be. Maybe it would be about organizational behavior or project management. Maybe today's would be about managing performance or appraisals, but it really didn't matter to me because these lessons were the kind you never could find in a book. There was no class syllabus, no report card, no summer break and no graduation; just class every day from 4:30 pm to 5:30 pm featuring lessons based on real-life experiences.

The teacher was neither an academic nor an adjunct; he didn't hold a certificate or an actual license to teach. But he did hold an important title, and he did wield a lot of influence. We never had to call him sir, mister or professor; he only went by one name, and that was Dad. He held class not in a room with a blackboard and erasers but rather in one with place settings and glasses. The greatest lessons of my life took place at our family

> "Often in life, the greatest lessons are taught by those who did not know they were teaching." – Fred Daum

dinner table as my father Fred Daum related the work day's events. He did not come home purposefully to teach. In his eyes, he was just recounting the day's events, but in my eyes, he was teaching the greatest lessons in the world. Often in life, the greatest lessons are taught by those who did not know they were teaching.

Photo 12-2: 1967, my dad and me

We lived in a small blue-collar town in New Jersey on the Delaware River across from South Philadelphia. From the banks of the river, we could look into Philadelphia and see Veterans Stadium where the Eagles played, watch the planes appear to touch the water as they landed at the airport, and if we looked to our left, we could see the towers and tanks of the oil refinery where my father worked rise up above the trees. The smell of the refinery was palpable along with the sounds it produced. From our home, you could hear the whistle of the refinery at 3:30 pm signaling there was a half hour left in the work day. At 4:00 pm, the whistle signaled that the day was over for the men who performed very dangerous work to provide for their families. But to me it signaled something different; it signaled class was going to start, that soon I would be able to listen to my father recount all the day's events, what dangerous jobs they performed, what conflicts arose and what problems were solved.

Photo 12-3: My father in his Marine uniform

If the school of hard knocks ever provided a graduation diploma, my father would have one hanging on the wall. My father grew up in Camden, New Jersey, in a small brick row home at the base of the Walt Whitman Bridge. To say that he was disadvantaged would be a gross understatement. At the age of nine, he was cooking for himself and his sister. After ninth grade he dropped out of school, and at fifteen he was working on a tracker trailer hauling and unloading Campbell's soup cases between Camden and New York City. At seventeen, he entered the United States Marine Corps and served four years where he received his

General Equivalency Diploma. He took great pride in being a Marine, and he would very quickly remind anyone who asked that he was not a "retired" Marine but rather an "inactive" Marine, ready to serve at a moment's notice and keeping himself in shape by performing a thousand pushups every other day. Eventually, he landed a job at the Texaco oil refinery as a ditch digger. There was no lower rung on the ladder, no lower entry level position and no other place to go but up.

Photo 12-4: My father and mother

Over the next 20 or so years, as my father strode through the front door at the end of the work day, our family would be sitting at the dinner table waiting for him to assume his position at the head of the table. Each day he would recount how hard he worked, what lessons he learned, and as days gave way to years, the promotions he received and the added responsibilities he gained. The ditch digger became a welder, then he became a pipe fitter, then he worked his way up to a welding shop fabricator; each step of the way talking about how he prepared for the next job opportunity, the next test, and how hard work always pays off. Over time, the high school dropout assumed a leadership position in the union and then on one of the most memorable days ever, he walked through our front door in a blue hard hat. That blue hard hat signified a new chapter of learnings, as he had accepted a job as an area supervisor. The lessons at the table moved to much more complicated topics such as performance management, setting expectations, discipline and development. My father was learning these lessons himself on the fly and often stumbling along the way. There was nothing that prepared him

Photo 12-5: My family in Colorado

for such a radical change of responsibilities. As he learned, I learned, and as he succeeded, I succeeded, because we were in this together every day from 4:30 pm to 5:30 pm. My father continued to advance his career into the realm of those who had college and engineering degrees, becoming a maintenance superintendent for the whole refinery. This presented a new set of challenges for him, as he was the man with all the field experience and practical knowledge working along-side the refinery academics. We negotiated these waters together, learn-ing how to communicate effectively and be a leader of men. Eventually, these lessons moved from the dinner table to the coffee shop and mall. We would walk and talk for hours about work; it was a bond we shared, a commonality between a father and a son. I am privileged to have gained years of work experience vicariously through him. These lessons remain an invaluable tool for me and have become the foundation upon which I have built my own leadership style.

> "Never underestimate how much influence you have and how fleeting time can be." – Fred Daum

The cornerstone of that foundation is all those lessons at the dinner table but not in the obvious way. Each of those lessons does influence my decision-making every day, but nothing has had more influence than the concept of what was really happening at our dinner table. My father was not intentionally teaching lessons but rather relating his satisfactions and dissatisfactions. He spoke about what his boss did well and didn't do so well, and he let us know how work impacted his dignity and self-esteem both pos-itively and negatively. This has driven me to ask myself: How do I influence what my team relates to their families at their dinner tables, over coffee or walking through the mall? Would it be recounting positive experiences, support and self-actualization opportunities? Or would it be an endless list of mundane tasks completed without purpose, creating no distinction between the end of one day and the start of another? Would they relate how hard work has paid off for them or would they say it is not worth the effort? Most importantly how would their experiences on my team frame their children's view of the work place? Would they talk about how work can be a satisfying part of one's life, where accomplishments and goals met can be celebrated? Or would they pass on that work is a just means to an end, the necessary funding of life's other more pleasurable activities?

> "Measure your success through their success."
> – Fred Daum

I call these questions my "Dinner Table Litmus Test." This simple test measures my leadership effectiveness by how I influence, positively or neg-atively, my team members' experiences at work. I imagine them relating those experiences at home to their family in the same manner my father related his experiences to me. I challenge myself to ensure that they are positive experiences and constantly improve my skills if they are not. It is not the most complex leadership style, but its effectiveness lies in its simplicity. Focus on removing obstacles, make their jobs easier rather than harder and measure your success through their success. When those things happen, the conversations at dinner are engaging and full of positive life lessons.

Photo 12-6: My father

On July 6, 2003, the refinery life that so influenced my father and me had one more tough lesson to teach. On that day, my mother called to tearfully let me know an accident occurred at the oil refinery in Aruba where my father was leading a workforce of 1,200 men. Tragically, my father was killed at work that day performing a dangerous job that he would not entrust to others. There would be no more conversations at the dinner table, talks over coffee or walks though the mall. But, as time is the greatest healer of all wounds, my anger has given way to forgiveness and my loneliness to gratitude. I was privileged to sit at the dinner table with one of the greatest teachers of all time, and I want him to know that no other person has had a more positive influence on me in my life. To honor his legacy, I work every day trying to pass the "Dinner Table Litmus Test," and I would encourage you to do the same. Never underestimate how much influence you have and how fleeting time can be.

Thanks, Dad for all the lessons and providing me opportunities you never had.

Your loving son, Freddie

PSEG Long Island is committed to building an industry leading electric company dedicated to providing the people of Long Island and The Rockaways with exceptional customer service, best-in-class reliability and storm response, and a strong level of involvement in the communities in which its employees live and work. Fred Daum is PSEG Long Island's Director of Customer Contact and Billing.

CHAPTER 13

JILL DOUCETT
Director, Customer Relations
NB Power

Photo 13-1: Jill Doucett

My grandfather, Talmadge "Sharkey" Clarke, is someone to whom I give credit for teaching me the lesson of letting people learn things themselves in their own way. I have a distinct memory of doing a task that was given to my little brother, hoping that I would be given credit for my initiative. But alas, I was chastised for taking the opportunity away from my brother, whether he would have done it or not and the learning that would have come from that, i.e. taking accountability. I think I've applied that lesson to my children as well as my employees. Perhaps not always consciously, but when I reflect on

Photo 13-2: Talmadge "Sharkey" Clarke, my grandfather with my grandmother

> Let people learn things themselves in their own way.
> — Jill Doucett

how important I believe it is for people to learn things in their way, I'd have to go back to that time with my grandfather.

"In order to build trust, which is paramount to the relationship, one must feel recognized, included, respected, and their self-esteem preserved." – Jill Doucett

---

Photo 13-3: Paul Theriault, my then boss and vice president of human resources

I worked in Human Resources for many years before moving to Customer Service. My boss, Paul Theriault, the vice president of Human Resources, taught me many lessons that have served me well in Customer Service. The HR strategy he espoused had some fundamental principles that still resonate with me when I'm dealing with people, whether employees or customers. In order to build trust, which is paramount to the relationship, one must feel recognized, included, respected, and their self-esteem preserved. From there, we could focus on the customer, on corporate excellence and teamwork to accomplish some great things. I've used these principles successfully in many circumstances, both business and personal, and think of him when I do. He recently passed away but has certainly left a legacy with those of us who had the opportunity to work with him.

During my career I've had many managers who have all taught me something, whether good or bad. One particular manager, with me in my first official supervisor role, was great at giving me opportunities to learn and grow. I was keen and interested in trying new things, and he was very supportive, agreeing to my suggestions. I learned however that despite his "support," he was putting safety nets in place for me rather than having a constructive discussion about the pros and cons of implementing some of those suggestions. My key learning from this experience is the importance of having a constructive and frankly honest discussion among team members as we consider strategies, examining the potential upsides and downsides. This requires having trust within the team to be able to do this to preserve an innovative spirit balanced with realistic perspective of success.

Consider the importance of constructive, frank and honest discussion when evaluating strategies and examining potential upsides and downsides. – Jill Doucett

---

There are many lessons in life. Thank you, mentors for your contributions to my journey through leadership!

Jill Doucett is NB Power's Director, Customer Relations. Headquartered in Fredericton, Canada, NB Power is the primary electrical utility in the Canadian province of New Brunswick. With 394,000 customers, NB Power's service philosophy focuses on customer interaction, market development, account management and energy counsel. They pride themselves on constantly improving call centre capacity and customer information technology to help deliver an "Easy To Do Business With" service strategy.

CHAPTER 14

DANA DRYSDALE
Vice President – Information Systems
San Jose Water

Photo 14-1: Dana Drysdale

I was very lucky growing up. There were mentors everywhere – teachers, coworkers and classmates. Really, the entire town helped form my values, but the two at the top of the pile are Ray and Ruth Drysdale, my dad and mom.

The earliest lesson I remember is a funny one. A piece of garden equipment would not start, so Ray and Ray Sr. gave me, a 4-year-old, an opportunity. They let me check the motor for spark by pulling the spark plug wire from the plug and trying to start the little motor. Bam, was there spark! After I stopped screaming, far more than necessary, Dad and Grandpa showed me how to be more careful. If I was going to help at Grandpa's shop and work with Dad around electricity, it was important to be safe. When it was time to start working away from the two Rays, I traded time helping at Grandpa's shop for use of the tractor to mow bigger lots in town. Other jobs followed in what seemed like a surprising way. Thanks to the two Rays, I started to understand risk, safety, barter and negotiation.

Photo 14-2: Ruth and Ray Drysdale
with Cousin Elizabeth Franklin

My dad Ray built many things with me – two computers, electronic testing equipment, a sound system, a television for our home. He taught me to read electrical schematics and much more. When my sister and I got into music, Dad and Mom paid for lessons until we could do so. When he needed to learn how to work with digital technology to stay relevant at work, Ray would head to our basement after dinner and study. Lifelong learning and the value of encouragement – looks like I learned that first from Dad.

Ruth, my mom, volunteered a lot, including starting and chairing a nonprofit day care. She was also an elementary school teacher and had me help her organize the classroom for many years. It seemed impossible to begin a school year with 30 third or fourth graders without being organized and ready to go. When I was older and visited her class, I remember Mom being calm in chaos and her ability to share knowledge through stories and examples. Mom's organization skills and approach to her work served as a valuable example for work and community service.

Some of the lessons learned were not evident until much later in our own family. Our kids participated in athletics. We volunteered to help with Little League, Swim Club, Rotary projects and high school and college sports. It just seemed to be the thing to do. Today, it seems obvious

Photo 14-3: Ray Drysdale and family with Cousin Sue

that we learned how to volunteer and encourage our children's activities from our parents. From Dad, I learned about working together on computers and electronics. If I needed to be a mechanic, whether making tools out of duct tape, old junk or whatever or talking with customers, I thank Grandpa for his early lessons.

Keep the three-legged "stool" in balance: customers, employees, shareholders. – Dana Drysdale

---

Most of my career is as part of the team at San Jose Water, and it seems everyone can always teach me something. I joined knowing little about the details of the business, how to get along in the company or how decision-making happened in the utility, so I learned from everyone - meter readers, engineers, operators and more. I still hope to learn something from these teachers every day.

One guy at San Jose Water made a big impression on our work and had a unique way of teaching a few simple lessons. Rich Roth, our recently retired CEO, believed that technology could make a big difference and insisted that we plan and measure those differences. The employee team used tech to change much about how things got done to improve service to customers, make work better for employees, and be more efficient.

One of my favorite Rich-isms is the three-legged stool and that the utility – the stool – will fall over unless we do right by its three legs: the customers, the employees and the stakeholders. One time, I

Photo 14-4: Rich Roth, the author of Rich-isms

had two coworkers on the team who went everywhere doing everything together, taking about the same amount of time one would alone. Time for a quote from the Montana ranch from Rich's dad, "When I sent you two hands out there riding fence, if you were supposed to work the same fence, I woulda put you on one horse." Smoothed up a bit, that one saying did the trick. The larger lesson is that little changes can make big differences in efficiency, and a little humor and story might help make change and communication happen.

"Know what you are working with before proceeding." – Dana Drysdale

---

CS Week is an important influence on me. When the SJW team needed to know what to consider in a catastrophe, colleagues I have met through CS Week's Executive Summit and Conference were valuable resources. Colleagues who learned to succeed through Hurricane Sandy and other natural disasters generously shared their careful planning, experience and wisdom. We used this knowledge to help develop our Emergency Response Plans and to create a special customer website for catastrophes. We hope we never have to use these crisis tools, but, if we do, we know some of the content is battle tested, thanks to our CS Week colleagues. We contribute, and we receive so much from association with CS Week colleagues. Sharing the right way always pays off.

Photo 14-5: My father-in-law John Marsh and me

It would be a terrible omission to leave out my father-in-law, John Marsh, CEO of the former Marsh Company of Belleville, Illinois. This man was blessed to be CEO of a small family business - about 60 employees - that grew to around 500 people. What I watched him do many times is convince his Board to try a new product for a small amount of funds. These products were modest successes, some hilarious failures and one huge success. John and his team knew what they were risking and never stopped trying. John also arranged unforgettable family outings. John Marsh taught me to always look for new ideas (John made it look fun and laughed at his stuff that didn't work), and he reinforced doing things as a family, from a picnic at the lake to hiking in Alaska.

"Little changes add up to a lot." – Dana Drysdale

Some of my mentors' lessons fell into the "do not emulate" category. Here is one example. At another company, I was working at a customer site and my boss asked me to get something done that afternoon. I knew it could not be done because it was too much work, and I told him so. "No problem," he said, "just ask the customer for some help." Before long, I had every customer resource working on the project. This ground to an abrupt halt when one of the company officers walked through the area. I just missed being fired that day. The lesson I learned: Ask first before enlisting help.

Summed up in a few lines, these bits of wisdom I received are astonishing and incredibly humbling:

- Know what you are working with before proceeding.
- Understand risk and safety.
- Keep learning and encourage creativity and learning.
- Get organized, and when the chaos comes, stay calm.
- Make good use of what you already have.
- Listen to the customers.
- Offer and reach a fair exchange of value.
- Learn from everyone.
- Always respect, refer to and recognize others.
- Find stuff that makes a difference and plan and measure results.
- Think about the impact on everyone and everything – especially customers, coworkers and shareholders.
- Little changes add up to a lot.
- Stay in good humor!
- Listen to stories and use stories to improve communication.
- Share knowledge and you will receive more than your share back.
- Take measured risks, make mistakes and laugh at them.
- Celebrate success!
- Create and support fun time with your family and friends.
- Be enthusiastic, but, if you need to borrow resources, be sure to ask first.

And, like most people, writing about a few life lessons makes me realize there are so many more mentors who continue to have a tremendous positive impact on my life. If I could send a letter to my mentors, it would say:

Dear coworkers, colleagues, mentors and family,
Thank you for what you taught me and are teaching me every day. It is not possible for me to repay you in any way that comes close to the value received. Every day, I apply the lessons you taught me. Because of what you did for me, I try to make the future better than today. When possible, I share the knowledge and wisdom you so

freely invested your time in giving me and many others. Above all, we try to have a good time. Things are going incredibly well.

Thank you,
Dana

Founded over 150 years ago, San Jose Water, an investor-owned public utility, is one of the largest and most technically sophisticated urban water systems in the U.S. It serves high quality, life-sustaining water to over one million people with an emphasis on exceptional customer service. SJW also provides operations and maintenance, billing and backflow testing services to other utilities, which benefit the local community, lower the cost of water operations and improve opportunities. As Vice President, Information Systems, Dana Drysdale is responsible for developing SJW's IT strategy and capabilities and delivering IT services.

CHAPTER 15

SHARON GROVE
Assistant General Manager, Customer Service Division
Los Angeles Department of Water and Power

Photo 15-1: Sharon Grove

I will never forget the boss I had who employed a Jekyll and Hyde management style – no one knew which person they would get from one day to the next. This boss believed that they were creating a sense of urgency, but instead they were creating an atmosphere where employees were always waiting for the other shoe to drop. Seeing how that style of management impacted the team, I resolved that I would avoid those mistakes when I became a manager. Instead, I aimed to be consistent and to be a servant leader every day. A big part of servant leadership is to create an environment where people aren't thinking about anything but their team, the customer and their work products. I knew that to build a strong team would create a productive work environment where people could achieve things they never thought possible and would give them a safe space to push their limits.

"'To get from point A to point B, you shouldn't expect to go in a straight line.'" – Sharon Grove

Pushing my own limits was a lesson that I learned early in life and from an unexpected source: basketball. I was always involved in sports, having participated in track and swimming from an early age, but I had never picked up a basketball until I was a high school sophomore faced with participating in a winter sport. I decided on basketball, figuring that, if nothing else, I would get to spend time with my best friend, who was also on the team.

> "Sometimes taking a little longer to achieve the end result gives everyone time to be on the same journey together. It makes change much smoother and easier to adopt."
> – Sharon Grove

As could be expected, I wasn't very good at first. In fact, I spent most games watching from the bench. As I watched, I was unable to suppress my naturally competitive spirit. I knew that I could be just as good as the girls who were out on the court and so, instead of feeling bad about warming the bench, I used that time to study them closely and apply what I learned during practice. The key was to be ready the second the opportunity happened, and the coach gave me the nod to "get in there." Fast forward two years, and I went from warming the sophomore bench to being a starter on the varsity team my senior year.

Playing basketball for my very determined and strong-willed varsity coach was an experience, to say the least. I had never been so exhausted, yet simultaneously exhilarated and proud of myself as I was after finishing the first practice. And it never got easier either, so my teammates and I just focused on finishing one practice at a time. The coach tried to pit us against each other, and he ran us until we were sometimes physically sick. But instead of competing against each other, we rallied together and rooted for one another as the season progressed. We became strong together, and we reached the state final for the first time in school history.

> "Career success is about enjoying what you do every day you are at work." – Sharon Grove

I went on to play for the women's basketball team at Lehigh University and then to play in a professional league in Europe. Basketball was the foundation for my self-awareness, self-confidence and coachability. The small wins I got along the way became the fuel driving me toward even more audacious goals. I didn't realize it at the time, but my coach was teaching me life lessons.

I held onto these life lessons as I moved through my career. When I became a manager, I was a results and action-oriented manager, often trying to push through obstacles to deliver. I reported to a CEO who took me into her office and sat me down for a discussion. She was very professional and reserved. She shared with me a valuable lesson that someone had taught her: to get from point A to point B, you shouldn't expect to go in a straight line. She used the analogy of a crab moving sideways over and over to make forward progress. In other words, sometimes taking a little longer to achieve the end result gives everyone time to be on the same journey together. It makes change much smoother and easier to adopt.

Over the years, I have passed on the benefits of moving less pointedly towards a goal to those whom I've mentored. With this and other lessons, I hope to better equip my employees for their career success. And by success, I don't merely mean advancement. Career success is about enjoying what you do every day you are at work, and the advancement often comes as a byproduct. I am grateful for the valuable life lessons that these individuals gave me.

Los Angeles Department of Water and Power is the largest municipal utility in the United States, serving over four million residents. Sharon Grove serves as Assistant General Manager, Customer Service Division, where she is responsible for overseeing customer operations across the electric and water service territory including call center, credit and collections, premier account management, customer programs for energy efficiency and water conservation, customer policy and technology. She is responsible for directing and positioning customer experience strategies, aligning business processes, understanding market and customer insights, and aligning customer contact channel strategies including customer self-serve initiatives, customer research and customer complaint resolution.

CHAPTER 16

MICHAEL GUYTON
Senior Vice President, Chief Customer Officer (Retired)
Oncor Electric Delivery

Photo 16-1: Michael Guyton

Two strong mentors provided me guidance and examples as I grew in my role and responsibilities at what is now known as Oncor Electric Delivery, Texas's largest electric transmission and distribution utility. Charles Lee was the Region Manager of our East Texas Region. I was a young manager who was trying to put a proposal together and had intentionally left off some of the critical facts that could possibly impact the decision out of my favor. Charles, by asking some basic questions, knew really fast what I was doing but graciously gave me an out so that I could confess what I had done. I apologized and committed to him and every manager that I reported to since that I would present all the facts, regardless of whether they hindered or supported my position. Credibility and trust take a lifetime to

"Credibility and trust take a lifetime to earn but can be lost in
a few words or no words at all." – Michael Guyton

earn but can be lost in a few words or no words at all. I desired then and still want to be known as a man of my word who can be trusted regardless of the circumstances.

Photo 16-2: One of my key mentors, Brenda Jackson

Brenda Jackson was our first Chief Customer Officer, and I worked for her a couple of times. Brenda absolutely loved people and saw the good in them. She was, however, stern in her approach to discipline and doing things right and the right way. While she did not say it in these words, the next phrase reflects what I have tried to leave to young managers: Praise in public and punish in private. I look for opportunities to catch my employees performing well, praising them in front of peers, their managers or my boss. And when they do things that need to be corrected, public shaming is something I never do (unless the conduct or behavior involves an imminent safety danger). I try to take them aside and let that event be a teaching moment or kick in the pants if necessary.

"Praise in public and punish in private." – Michael Guyton

Most of us are uncomfortable at performance reviews and having those tough conversations. While delivering the raise with a wink-and-a-nod and the unspoken message, 'just keep doing what you're doing,' is easier, employees want and deserve more so they can grow and develop to their fullest potential. If readers find themselves in this situation like I did, let me offer some friendly advice: Put together a list of accomplishments for the year along with your goals for the upcoming year and take that to your boss for discussion. The boss and you are now working from your list and documents. I considered performance reviews as an opportunity to take my personal development in my hands. I now have each of my direct reports do the same thing. We go over their last year accomplishments, set next year's goals and objectives and agree to a personal development plan. Performance reviews are now fun.

"Put together a list of accomplishments for the year along with goals for the upcoming year and take that to your boss for discussion. The boss and you are now working from your list and documents." – Michael Guyton

---

If I could reach back over the decades, I would tell Charles Lee, "Thank you for not being too harsh on me and giving me a second chance." I have never made that mistake again. Instead, I have spent the last 40 years doing things the right way and for the benefit of the customers, the company and the employees, never for my own benefit. I have been incredibly blessed because of that second chance. Also, I would tell Brenda Jackson, "Thanks for letting your boss know all of my successes and kicking me in the pants when I needed it." I would tell her, "I tried to pass it on," and am grateful for being given the opportunity.

Michael Guyton wore many hats in various leadership roles across his 40-year career with the sixth largest US utility, Oncor Electric Delivery. He retired in June 2018 after six years as Senior Vice President, Chief Customer Officer. Serving more than 10 million customers living in 401 Texas cities and 91 counties, Oncor is more than just a utility service provider. Its 3,400 employees help Texans meet the challenge of rethinking energy use for greater efficiency, cost savings and positive environmental impact. Oncor partners with communities to support the environment, promote safety and teach consumers about electricity.

CHAPTER 17

VIC HATRIDGE
Chief Information Officer (Retired)
Nashville Electric Service

Photo 17-1: Vic Hatridge

My dad was my first mentor. He was uneducated and unsophisticated, but he taught me invaluable life lessons. We all had assigned chores at home and were expected to finish our work before we did any playing. Also, as poor country folks, my dad had learned many life skills including farming/gardening, auto mechanics, carpentry, plumbing, welding, etc. I learned many of those basic skills from him

"The most important lessons I learned from my dad were about honesty and integrity. We learned at an early age to live within our means, to take care of what little we had and to always pay our debt."
– Vic Hatridge

Photo 17-2: My dad Robert with my sisters Janis and Mary in 1942

Avoid paralysis by analysis. – Vic Hatridge

and continue to use them. But, the most important lessons I learned from my dad were about honesty and integrity. We learned at an early age to live within our means, to take care of what little we had and to always pay our debts. I have lived my entire life by those standards.

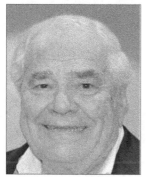

Photo 17-3: Don Baker, the man at Arthur Anderson & Co. who set my career on its path

Don Baker of Arthur Andersen & Co. in Houston was the man who gave me my first job out of college. Don was not really a mentor, but he set my career on its path. Sure, I had a college degree, even an MBA, but I was so dumb when I interviewed with Don. I was immature and socially inept, a true country bumpkin. But somehow, Don saw potential in me and hired me. I spent eleven years there and received lots of formal and on-the-job training in this new thing called "management information systems." I developed consulting skills and people skills and improved my writing and speaking skills tremendously. I learned to lead and motivate others. My time there formed the foundation of my entire professional life.

"'If you enjoy your job, you'll never work a day in your life.'" – Vic Hatridge

Photo 17-4: My mentor at Nashville Electric Service, Dr. Matthew Cordero

Dr. Matthew Cordero hired me as Chief Information Officer at Nashville Electric Service some years later. Interestingly enough, my background with Arthur Andersen & Co. was what impressed him most. The key lesson I learned from him was to get away from analysis paralysis. I needed to make decisions and take actions; that is what others were looking for from me. I believe I became much more effective and certainly enjoyed my job more when I made that change.

One boss told me that we work only to earn enough money to enable us to do the things we really want to do outside of work. I could never accept the idea that a job had to be something I just tolerated. I wanted to enjoy my job and the people I worked with, so I always tried to bring this same enjoyment

Photo 17-5: This Rwandan gorilla and I were certainly enjoying our jobs that day.

to those who worked for and with me. Like they say, "If you enjoy your job, you'll never work a day in your life." I think all leaders should strive for this.

To my dad – thank you, and I am sorry I never told you how much you did for me. By the way, I have always paid all my debts.

To Don Baker – thank you for hiring a country bumpkin. How did you know what I could accomplish?

To Matthew Cordero – thank you for the stability of the utility job you gave me. As a result, I was able to be home most every night and participate deeply in raising my children.

Distributing energy to more than 385,000 customers in middle Tennessee, Nashville Electric Service (NES) is one of the 12 largest public electric utilities in the nation. It remains committed to three service pillars: providing reliable power, staying safe around electricity and protecting the environment. NES is among only four percent of all public utilities in the country to receive the Reliable Public Power Providers Diamond Award, the industry's highest honor for offering safe and reliable electricity to customers. Vic Hatridge served as its Chief Customer Officer for over 20 years, retiring in 2014. Vic now serves as the CS Week venue executive for LeadNext.

CHAPTER 18

CHRIS LAIRD
Executive Director – Electric Operations
Consumers Energy

Photo 18-1: Chris Laird

My parents come from different parts of the country. My mother was born and raised in Louisiana and my father in Michigan. As a result, I remember listening to my parents talk about their point of view from two very different perspectives. This early life lesson taught me to have an open mind and listen as a way to seek understanding, which I've applied as both a mentee and mentor over my career. My father also coached most of my sports as a young athlete and focused on a few key aspects that I've carried with me since a young age.

First, be proud of your work ethic. You rarely get anything handed to you in life and hard work, done the right way, results in new opportunities that others may not get. Second, be a great teammate. Be supportive of your team members as they all have something positive to contribute. Encouraging others and recognizing them for things done well can result in an increase in performance. Lastly, be willing to try things you don't like. Everyone on the team wants to be the point guard or the top scorer, but teams need great defenders and rebounders too. Use your strengths to take on opportunities that make the team stronger. The lessons I learned at a young age through these examples taught me to not focus on "what's in it for me" but to pay attention to on how I can improve and support those around me.

Fast forward a decade and I'm starting my career. I've been assigned a mentor but really have no idea what this means or how to proceed. Ironically, the mentor that's been assigned to me has even less of an idea about how we should handle this relationship, so we set up monthly meetings and mainly talked about golf. When I attempted to discuss work, I was given the not too helpful advice to ask my supervisor. While I appreciated having a senior leader to communicate with, I really didn't see the value in the mentor/mentee relationship and reluctantly ended up asking for a reassignment. I only tell this story to share that this was one of the biggest learning opportunities that I've ever had over my career and has shaped how I handle being both a mentee and mentor today. I vowed from that day forward to ensure clear expectations were set and that "we" agreed on agenda items and how to proceed for all future communications.

"Have an open mind and listen as a way to seek understanding." – Chris Laird

---

Insert my new mentor, a bright and energetic leader who works in a completely different area of the company with vast experience outside of the utility as well. She appreciated my organization and structure to our meetings (learned from my last failure), and I appreciated her ability to listen and provide guidance without giving direction. My new mentor would take notes as I discussed various topics and would ask questions to further the discussion. I would randomly get a book delivered to my office with a note saying, "Read this highlighted chapter," which was based on our last mentoring conversation. Her ability to enhance my development in various ways was a breath of fresh air. I went from dreading my mentoring conversations to craving the next time we met. We never spoke of golf once.

At the same time, I was assigned my new mentor, I received an opportunity to become a mentor for a newer employee. This high-level individual contributor was looking to move to a leadership role, and management paired us up given my background of leadership progression. I was excited and eager to start this relationship and find ways to enhance the development of my new mentee. One thing I learned quickly was that we had very different backgrounds, which resulted in different views on how we could proceed with development. I leveraged the methods my mentor taught me but had to reflect on my personal leadership and development. In a few of my previous roles, I had the privilege to work for a few outstanding leaders. One of my former leaders had an operational background, was data-focused and continuously challenged our team to identify the root cause for issues. This was done to make permanent corrections that would best serve our peer teams who counted on us to deliver. This same leader encouraged me to reach out to peers and work through challenges which resulted in an expanded network that I still leverage today. The leader I worked for directly after that had a completely different background, one in human resources and customer operations. This leader taught me to focus on the people and our customers. Without even realizing it, I now had an understanding of how to leverage my network of resources, understand the impact of our employees and keep the focus of the discussion on positive customer results. As a new mentor, I was able to pull nuggets of wisdom that I learned previously and provide recommendations for areas of development for my new mentee.

"Be willing to try things you don't like." – Chris Laird

Let people learn from your mistakes! I've taken risks over my career, enjoying some success but making plenty of mistakes along the way. I now mentor ten employees around the company, two formally and eight informally. As I listen to them work through their challenges, I've learned to share personal stories about mistakes I've made and how I would handle it differently in the future. I've found that the tremendous talent, my mentees, truly appreciates me sharing "real world" examples of challenges that I've faced throughout my personal life and career.

Photo 18-2: Laird family

Every opportunity is a chance to develop through a form of mentorship. My wife also works for a large company and experiences similar challenges to what we all face working for utilities. My wife and I use each other as sounding boards on almost a daily basis, sometimes

Photo 18-3: Family Christmas morning on Lake Michigan

intentionally and other times not even realizing we are doing it. We also have two wonderful children, a freshman in high school and a fifth grader. It's amazing how intelligent kids are today, and I've found through my extensive trips around the Midwest for travel soccer that my kids are actually really great people from which to get opinions. My daughter fights through relationship challenges on a daily basis, some not much different than what we face at work. I'll ask her how she handled situations, or she'll ask me for advice. Getting an outside reference is very refreshing, and you might be very surprised to the similarities in experiences you and your kids have.

In every role I've had throughout my career, I've had the pleasure to directly interact with customers. My past experiences have taught me to listen to customers, work hard to correct mistakes when they occur and to work even harder to prevent mistakes from occurring in the first place. I'll use the feedback from the customer and take their "voice" back to our operating teams to enhance customer service levels. I've learned to play all the positions on the court, including being a coach at times and giving tremendous effort to ensure success for our customers. Most importantly, I'll continue to develop via my mentoring relationships. My advice is to remain open in your development and share your experiences with others, so they can learn as they build their own path and career growth.

"Work hard to correct mistakes when they occur and… work even harder to prevent mistakes from occurring in the first place." – Chris Laird

---

Lastly, I'm a liaison with one of our largest customers and have established a trusted relationship with the president of the company and his team. He randomly calls me and asks me to fill in as a fourth on their golf scramble along with his two sons. I guess my first mentor's golf advice paid off after all.

To my mentors, family, friends, coworkers and customers, I say, "Thank you."

My goal, in every situation, is that we leave it better than we found it, and I've never been more confident that we're headed in the right direction.

Headquartered in Jackson, MI, Consumers Energy was voted in July 2018 by Cogent Reports, a division of Marketing Strategies International, as a "Most Trusted Brand." This ranks CE in the top 15 in the nation among providers of electricity and natural gas according to business customers. The state's largest energy provider, CE provides natural gas and electricity to 6.7 million residents in all 68 Lower Peninsula counties. It is also ranked by *Forbes* magazine as Michigan's best place to work and recognized nationally for its commitment to providing job opportunities to military veterans. Chris Laird is its Executive Director – Electric Operations.

CHAPTER 19

EVA M. LIGGINS
Director of Operations
DC Office of Tax and Revenue

Photo 19-1: Eva M. Liggins

Two independent women played influential roles in my girlhood years growing up in Petersburg, Virginia. The first was the school librarian hired by the elementary school I attended after she completed her student teaching semester. Mrs. Ruth Morgan-Hairston set ablaze the love of learning for me with a library of books and her personal encouragement. I volunteered in the library as a young student after school and during the summers. During those hours together, she taught me to be intellectually curious and to seek knowledge, both goals achievable within those four walls lined with books. She would have me locate specific books and read them, knowing they could expand my perspective and grow my small-town universe. Mrs. Hairston also suggested books appropriate for a maturing, curious girl like Louisa May Alcott's *Little Women*. During the summers, she allowed me to read to children enrolled in the library summer programs.

"Reading was essential for my success." – Eva M. Liggins

She understood that reading helped vocabulary and language development, sharpened grammar and punctuation skills and modeled good composition and sentence structure. But most of all, Mrs. Hairston realized books opened the world to an impressionable African-American girl growing up in the still segregated South in the 1960s. She understood reading was essential for my success.

"Always define the problem, organize the work, care about the people and pay attention to detail." – Eva M. Liggins

---

A couple of years ago, I searched Facebook to see if I could locate Mrs. Hairston, the librarian who gave me responsibility and made such an impression. Once we connected and became "friends," Mrs. Hairston posted two pictures she had saved of me in the third grade. I guess I made an impression on her, too.

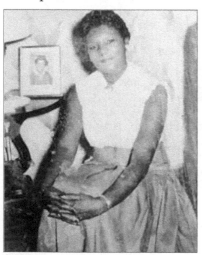

Photo 19-2: My Aunt Cille

The second woman who influenced me in lasting ways was my mother's sister, Aunt Lucille. Born in 1921, Aunt Lucille was what I affectionately call, "a Renaissance woman." Though she didn't finish high school, she reinforced the importance of education every day in many ways when I came to live with her in the fourth grade. In her home, I was exposed to a panorama of visual and performing arts and so many genres of music. Whether it was jazz or classical, blues or gospel, Aunt Lucille loved music, and she filled her home with it. An artist in her own right, Aunt Lucille drew and painted. She took me to theater performances, dance recitals and art exhibits. Married but with no children, Aunt Lucille lived as an independent woman while her husband lived and worked in New York. She made her own life in every way, and I was thankful to share it with her until I left for college. Aunt Lucille was the first and only African-American hair stylist in the Colonial Heights' beauty salon. She worked hard to become the first certified black stylist in the state of Virginia, an achievement that reinforced her lesson to me: pursue excellence in all that I do. I miss my Aunt Lucille; she was quite a woman and such a positive role model.

Once I finished college and started my career, one mentor stands out for the practical lessons I learned from him. H. Stan Hill was the manager for a private fleet management company in Hunt Valley, Maryland, where I worked for eight years. He taught me to always define the problem, organize the work, care about the people and pay attention to detail. But he was also innovative. Together, Stan and I created a new department called Shift Operations, an experiment to save time and money by creating a shift that performed day-to-day administrative work at night to free up the day shift, allowing them to focus on sales and service. Our experiment started with six people on the night shift and peaked four years later with 24-hour operations and a staff of 70. Stan engaged with me daily, holding me accountable, helping me establish productivity standards, paying attention to the work quality and creating service level agreements with other departments. A man of high character and a good husband and father, Stan taught me business administration fundamentals and allowed me to practice them with his oversight. All these lessons, I still use. We remain in contact even today.

> "'Just because you're poor doesn't mean you have to have an impoverished mind.'" – Eva M. Liggins

If I could write a letter to any of my mentors, I'd address it to my Aunt Lucille:

Dear Aunt Lucille,
Thank you for teaching me to face adversity and still maintain my dignity. Your impact and influence on me were profound and lasting. Thank you for instilling in me the importance of taking pride in my work, whatever it is, and helping me understand that my work reflects who I am. You taught me to be fearless and to not be intimidated – by anyone, especially during a time when you were not allowed to ride in the front of the bus and during an era when African-American women were treated as invisible and their opinions unwelcome. You always spoke up for yourself, and you taught me by your loving example. That courage has helped me face my own adversities. The sacrifice you made to raise me when my mother was overwhelmed as a single mother with six children is a witness to your sisterly love and your compassion in action. Your words, "Just because you're poor doesn't mean you have to have an impoverished mind," remain with me today. You

gave up what could have been a very different life to help raise me, and I'm forever grateful to you.

Your loving niece, Eva

Eva M. Liggins is the Director of Operations for DC Office of Tax and Revenue. Under the Office of the Chief Financial Officer, these operations are responsible for financial and budgetary functions of the District government and administering and enforcing the District's tax laws, collecting revenue for the city and recording deeds and other written instruments affecting a right, title, or interest in real or personal property in the District, among other oversight duties. Its online customer web portal, MyTax.DC.gov. offers consumers a safe, easy way to view and pay taxes.

CHAPTER 20

MICHAEL LOWE
*Deputy General Manager, Customer Operations and Services
& Chief Customer Executive (Retired)*
Salt River Project

Photo 20-1: Michael Lowe

Name a mentor that taught you key lessons at a young age. Describe those lessons. My parents. The overarching lesson I learned from my parents was the sustaining energy generated by a cohesive, loving family. My parents indelibly shaped my being with innumerable learnings: love of family and pride in family heritage; respect for others; appreciation of diversity in thought; perseverance and hard work; thoughtfulness; and humility. My father emphasized the importance of education and life-long learning. Together, they taught me to believe in myself, to trust my judgment and instincts and to find balance in both my work and personal life.

Appreciate the sustaining energy generated by a cohesive, loving family and pride of family heritage. – Michael Lowe

---

Photo 20-2: My most influential mentor, Therese Grayson, CEO, ProMeridian International

Name a mentor that taught you key lessons in your business career. Describe those lessons. Therese Grayson, CEO of ProMeridian International, Scottsdale, Arizona. Early in my career, my experience and skills were heavily weighted in Finance and IT. I enjoyed the analytical and logical approach to solving business issues and finding creative ways to deliver solutions. In 1994 as the utilities were facing the potential of deregulation, I was charged with leading SRP's Customer Operations. Transitioning a highly customized and aging customer information system while improving customer service proved to be a challenge: our existing team was understaffed and often lacked skills to be successful in a changing environment; our technology partnerships were strained; and our culture was very resistant to change.

I engaged Therese Grayson as my executive coach in 1998 to help me build our business, technology and vendor management skills. In addition, we needed definable, repeatable processes and tools that would allow our teams to consistently approach solution development and to successfully navigate our new culture. The coaching relationship continues to this day.

Understand the power of a written vision statement.
– Michael Lowe

One of the first lessons I learned from Therese was the power of a written vision statement. I worked with my team to craft a vision that challenged all of us to make service with SRP rewarding, easy and pleasant. That has been our overarching beacon now for 19 years and drives employee hiring and training, our policies, procedures and technologies.

We became laser focused on understanding and documenting our processes and practicing business resumption and disaster recovery. With Therese's counsel and encouragement, I introduced formal business process modeling methodologies and tools to SRP and reworked the processes from past eras to reduce complexity and cost and to make them responsive to customer needs.

I have learned to pace myself in changing culture, systems and processes. In short, I've learned to run a marathon rather than a continuous series of sprints. I take small bites at the apple, make smaller organizations within an organization and set them up to be successful. In working with Therese, we have focused on a handful of steps to meet my change-leadership goals. Success follows when I set the vision, provide the success parameters and give people permission to fail. In other words, I give them a safe environment to think and perform outside the box. Business processes are definable and repeatable allowing the rest of the organization to follow in a consistent manner. We don't fall in love with our process, knowing it will change over time, but we do celebrate the success along the way.

Describe key lessons that may have been well-intentioned by mentors but rightfully fell into the category of "Please don't emulate." Technology integration with business process is vital to our success. Over the years, many vendors and IT leaders have advised me to utilize their teams to identify potential solutions and implementation plans. In other words, let them do it for the business. I believe we have to have technology partners that work together with the business in order to ensure our success. What I have learned over the years is that vendors and IT need to know not only what we do, but how and why we do it in a particular way. You can have a technical installation be successful, but the business can be crippled for years if the installation doesn't support the business needs or workflow. System installation and business implementation are two separate and distinct efforts.

"Business processes are definable and repeatable allowing the rest of the organization to follow in a consistent manner. We don't fall in love with our process, knowing it will change over time, but we do celebrate the success along the way."
– Michael Lowe

What I have implemented that has significantly increased our successes is an integrated approach and a governance process that includes IT, vendors and my business experts. We integrate our teams and utilize our documented business processes and our analysts to ensure communication, training and organizational support thrive throughout all phases of the implementation. Having a holistic approach to identifying, implementing and supporting change is critical for our business success. We can no longer afford to let "others" lead efforts that impact our business. We need to be transformational in our thinking. Teams need to be educated and informed on both business and technical implications of change efforts, and we need to have a shared mindset on what success looks like for the company, not individuals, teams or vendors.

If you could write a letter to the mentors in 1, 2, or 3 above, what would you say. Therese, thank you for illuminating the many issues and opportunities for me over the years, and for your patience and commitment as I worked through understanding, acceptance and mastery of them. And, thank you for the thousands of hours of your time over the years in preparation for our meetings.

You have helped me to weave the diversity of talents within customer operations – the analytically-inclined employees, the procedure-focused staff, the emotionally-driven staff and the visionaries – into an extremely powerful force, not only within SRP, but within the utility industry.

And, you have been instrumental in assisting me in leveraging my background in finance and software development which I brought with me into this function into an enduring competitive advantage for SRP. There have been so many learnings with respect to: managing the politics, timing and communication of large system implementations; crafting business resumption plans in the event of system failures; classifying all customer system data elements to ensure availability, security and integrity; managing government grants; crafting cyber security plans well before they were an organizational norm at SRP; tightly governing the multiple concurrent initiatives we always seem to have underway; and developing the Customer Operations staff and preparing them for inevitable changes.

SRP's success and indeed my success, that is signified in SRP's 29 J.D. Power Awards for residential and business customer satisfaction, is also your success.

Salt River Project (SRP) is the oldest multipurpose federal reclamation project in the U.S., providing electric and water services to central Arizona since 1903. Today, as one of the nation's largest public power utilities, SRP provides electricity to one million residential and business customers. It is the largest water supplier to Phoenix's municipal, urban and agricultural water users. Retiring from an impressive, long career with SRP in June 2018, Michael Lowe has served in a variety of leadership positions in finance, information systems and customer services. He was its Deputy General Manager, Customer Operations and Services & Chief Customer Executive.

CHAPTER 21

JULIE LUPINACCI
Chief Customer Officer
Hydro Ottawa

Photo 21-1: Julie Lupinacci

If there is anything I have learned in my career it is this: leadership is not about me; it is about the people that are brave enough to follow and execute on an idea, concept or plan. Taking this notion a bit further, I would say my success is not my own; it is a culmination of experience, relationships and circumstance. Any success I have had through my life is thanks to so many people. Like any journey, there are hills and valleys, and I am grateful for each and every one. These experiences personify who I am, and they will continue to shape my future self... I can't wait to meet her!

Before I get too far ahead of myself, I want to acknowledge that too many women continue to encounter all types of friction in their lives. Preconceived interpretations of what a woman's path should be limit our collective potential. There are simply too many stories of women who have stopped dreaming, having bought into what others believe to be their full potential. I should disclose that I am privileged to have been surrounded by strong women and encouraging men, both at home and in business. If you take nothing else from my story, please hold onto this: **You are the driver of your life, You can achieve more than you know, and You deserve everything that you hope and dream for. So, go out and get it!**

"Leadership is not about me; it is about the people that are brave enough to follow and execute on an idea, concept or plan. Taking this notion a bit further, I would say my success is not my own; it is a culmination of experience, relationships and circumstance." – Julie Lupinacci

---

When I was a teenager, I worked for a grocery store that realized it had a problem with thievery. There was evidence suggesting that both customers and employees were stealing merchandise. To address the situation, the company implemented a policy that all staff, upon leaving their shift, was subject to physical search. Management checked our handbags, our backpacks, our person. Everyone was assumed guilty. Searches were conducted in the open where other employees and customers saw and assumed the worst. The message, "We don't trust you," screamed in my head as I and my workmates felt exploited. That policy really rubbed me the wrong way, but I didn't have the courage then to stand up. Management's mistreatment and invasion of privacy bothered me so much that I told my dad, a police officer. I knew he would understand my outrage because of his job; he knew and enforced personal privacy and property laws. Although this store's search policy may have been well-intentioned, management had failed to communicate effectively to staff or explain why they were doing it. My dad visited the store manager to share the perception that this practice emanated, and the search procedures quickly changed to provide the privacy that all deserved.

That situation still influences me today. I learned that to gain traction on change initiatives I needed to start from where others were standing and not rush in thinking that I know what's best for a situation, a person or an organization. This simple lesson has served me well throughout my career. In my early days as a project leader, working with a cross-functional team, getting a sense of where everyone was coming from, what they were bringing to the table (skillset, perceptions and preconceived notions), and what their goals were (personal and professional) allowed me to significantly reduce the ramp up time. Each team member bought into the project early and knowing that their goals were being considered ensured that they were vested in getting it done. More recently this philosophy helped me jump from one industry (print) to another (utility). When I joined Hydro Ottawa,

I started by listening, getting to know my team and observing/absorbing how and why they performed their functions. I learned what was working and what wasn't through their lenses. By appreciating where they'd been and why they had certain programs, procedures and policies, I was able to visualize what the path looked like from their vantage point and work with them to develop a plan (at times a bit of a different route) to get there. People are complex, so the key for me is to know where they come from and to appreciate their rich history and perspectives. I've found that once team members understand that the actions being implemented encompass their thoughts, processes and views, there is a higher level of engagement and overall success producing the best results.

Photo 21-2: My mom and dad, John and Germaine Gaudet

To understand how I see my present, it is best to know a bit of my past. Like many, my parents formed my first circle of influence. Together, John and Germaine Gaudet instilled the core beliefs that make me who I am today. My brothers and sister would likely nod their heads in agreement. Growing up together, we learned strong work ethics, a clear sense of doing the right things, and the importance of being honest in what we did and said. The elements were simple:

- Finish what you start.

- If you say you're going to do something, then follow through.

- Try new things.

They taught these lessons with everyday situations. Encouragement was the foundation in our household. Saying "No, you can't do that," or "You aren't allowed," wasn't part of their vocabulary. Rather, my mom and dad always asked us to think about how we would go about doing something. I remember being 16 years old and getting my '365,' which in Canada is a learner's driving permit, a big step towards every teenager's independence and freedom. My dad reminded me that I needed to take driving lessons, to earn the right to get behind the wheel. He continued, "You can't just go out and drive, you have to take a class to learn the skill and then practice it." That was how it was with John Gaudet: learn something and then repeat it until it became second nature. At 18, working and making money, another milestone

Photo 21-3: Mom and me in the car with sunrise or sunset in the windshield

became having my own car. My dad didn't say 'no' to my buying a car, even though he knew that I couldn't financially afford it, because discouraging me wasn't his style. Instead, he asked me to put a plan together to buy AND maintain the car. He insisted that the plan reflect the reality of my economic means, i.e. he wasn't subsidizing the purchase. That was his parenting style. He taught me how to look at situations through different angles, understand the impacts from all sides and encouraged me to strive for what I wanted by reaching for them with a well-constructed plan. I ended up not buying that car. It was hard at the time to admit my dad was right; so, I'll do that now – "Dad, you were right!" Not long after, I was able to put a successful plan together to purchase and maintain my own car. As you might expect, the same scenario played out when buying my first house, only I had a solid plan. When I reviewed it with my dad, he was proud to say I had thought of almost everything. Dad is always there sitting in the passenger seat to guide but not to steer. Being prepared has served me in many personal situations and so many more professionally. It is imperative to ask questions and not be afraid of the unknown. By rolling up my sleeves, doing some research, asking the experts for answers and not getting defensive, I've always found a way forward... thank you, due diligence!

My mom, Germaine, held a different but equal influence on our house-hold. I had the benefit of knowing her both as a stay-at-home mom and career woman in my childhood. She and my dad decided that when we moved to Ottawa, she would return to work. I observed her transition to the workforce and saw what that meant to our family with regards to the division of household responsibilities. There was no gender divide in the Gaudet home. My father cooked, did laundry, ironed and shared a thousand other household tasks with my mother. We kids pitched in too. The work was divided, and we all did our chores. From a young age, I saw how import-ant it was to contribute to the household, especially on those occasions when she brought work home. My parents showed us kids a strong work ethic, the importance of taking ownership for your assignments and collaborating to get things done. I am eternally grateful for all that my parents did for us, but I am especially proud to have had such a strong woman figure to call 'mom.'

She found a way to balance work and family. She encouraged me to have a voice and to speak up. She never accepted the phrase, "I can't" and insisted that I learn how if I sincerely thought that I couldn't. As such, my independence, my voice and my drive are thanks in large part to her.

> "To gain traction on change initiatives I needed to start from where others were standing and not rush in thinking that I know what's best for a situation, a person or an organization." – Julie Lupinacci

My parents had evolved from their parents' and grandparents' societal norm, "Children should be seen but not heard." In the Gaudet house, we were encouraged to share concepts and thoughts around the dinner table. We were asked our opinions and questioned about their inception and development. We were never shushed. This helped build my confidence to bring ideas and opinions forward, and a pivotal lesson taught by an aunt still guides me every day in my professional career. Sitting at the kitchen table, my aunt expressed frustration with one of her brothers and told my mother how it upset her that he often missed family events. She would say, "He's never here; he never shows up." Sitting there listening, I absorbed the conversation and responded, "Did you ever ask if he was available or ever seek his input on dates, activities or other details?" I added, "If he were asked to help plan events and activities, maybe he'd participate." My aunt paused for a moment and said, "I never thought of it like that." I am not privy to all that followed, but I do know that she and my uncle had a good discussion, and he has been to almost every family event since. This very short conversation (at least on my part) and the resulting action and impact it has had on our family have left its mark with me. I learned that even the most obvious things, to us, are sometimes obscured by one's perceptions and the filters and personal biases that they have. I realized that if we can refocus a situation or back away to see another perspective, we can often see a path in another direction that gets us to the end goal. This doesn't mean that all the steps are identified, only that when we shift our perspectives or help others do likewise, alternatives become visible.

I've had many great mentors after my parents, a notable one being a manager at a print and logistics firm with whom I worked for over 16 years. Under his tutelage, I witnessed first-hand the power of mentorship. This manager was my boss, so one could say it was his job to mentor me, but I've seen so many bosses not even touch that aspect of their jobs. His leadership style, at least with me, was empowering. He took time to understand what my professional goals and ambitions were. Armed with that insight, he was able to provide me opportunity after opportunity to work on projects and with customers that were truly exciting. I was always nervous about being pigeon-holed, and he did everything in his power to ensure that my path was as wide and deep as I wanted. I ended up working for him in different roles, despite my initial thoughts of this being a 6-month stint to gain experience. From project management, customer relationship management, sales and marketing to international trade relations, new program development and different managerial levels; my evolution was vast and progressive. My leadership style has evolved through the years, but my focus on helping team members strive and reach their full potential can largely be attributed to him.

> "Having a support system that can celebrate with you, lift you up, dust you off, and even at times set you straight is essential to achieving success in your life and in your career." – Julie Lupinacci

---

This manager also displayed a significantly different approach to the mantra, "The customer is always right." His philosophy of customer service was to offer a consultative approach tailored to each situation and individual customer. Rather than pushing a product or solution, he would listen, walk in our customers' shoes, understand their issues and appreciate what they truly wanted or needed. Then, he would draw parallels to see if we had solutions that fit. If we didn't, he told the customer we weren't the best solution, and we moved on. But if there was no right solution in the marketplace, and we had the resident skillset to help, we developed the solution tailored to that customer. This was a refreshing service approach. It allowed us to provide value-added services targeting individual customer needs. That mindset has followed me throughout my career. I've been privileged to be on teams that develop solutions which in many cases never existed. I've become comfortable addressing challenges where A + B doesn't always equal C. As such, my philosophy is that we should help people find solutions that deliver true value for them and not simply sell canned products and services. Developing those solutions on the fly empowers a workplace and engenders employee confidence. For example, when customers call Hydro Ottawa with high utility bills, those contacts open doors to proactively identifying what we can do to both reduce their bill and find new programs for home retrofits or other services. What an amazing opportunity to truly make a difference in the world of our customers.

Photo 21-4: My mass book photo

Looking at my bookshelf (stacked full and overflowing), I have to acknowledge that covers and spines are among my most influential mentors. Books have played a huge role in my professional development and elevated the traditional education achieved from college and university. I've done a lot of reading and attended many webinars and conferences. There, I learned and absorbed best practices, philosophies, methodologies and alternate management techniques. If I wasn't familiar with something or wanted to get into something new, my process was simple: go out and gain the skillset, close the gap with training. One conference speaker whose motivational message struck a chord was T. Harv Eker. He introduced the idea of "de-committing." The foundation to this is that many of us, me included, are raised to finish what you start. But what if what you started is the wrong thing to have started in the first place or no longer serves the right purpose? His concept was that one should formally de-commit and release the burden of "finishing it." That message is anathema in many organizations where the battle cry is 'Just finish the project.' Eker recognized that as we evolve the business, new technologies and offerings arise, and sometimes how you've done something or planned a program just doesn't make sense anymore. He emphasized that if a pursuit or objective or goal or project no longer serves you or your organization, or it doesn't provide the results you're looking for or need, it is okay to formally de-commit and drop it. In business, this lesson has been personally empowering because sometimes I've had to say, "Stop the presses! Hold on! We need to stop doing this and refocus on a different solution and move on past the previous one."

I would be remiss if I didn't acknowledge my husband, Claudio Lupinacci, as one of the most significant contributors to my life and to my evolving leadership style. Our

Photo 21-5: My husband Claudio and me

approach to situations (and people), although aligned in our values, is very different. It is not uncommon for us to have deep conversations about the day, and he inevitably highlights an area that I didn't consider. His perspective helps to curtail my blind spots (we all have them). He also reminds me about the best of humanity which is especially helpful on those days when I find myself swelled up in negativity. Claudio helps to anchor me in what's important, remind me that leadership has nothing to do with me, and that it's all about the people. Having a support system that can celebrate with you, lift you up, dust you off, and even at times set you straight is essential to achieving success in your life and in your career. I am so thankful to Claudio every day.

There are so many people that I would like to thank for helping me evolve into the leader that I am today, and I have only touched on a few here. I sincerely appreciate every person that I have encountered throughout my life, and all those that are yet to come. The letter to my mentors may be short, but it is forged deep in my heart.

"Your influence has had impacts on my personal and professional life in more ways than you will ever know. I hope that I am able to emulate and embody at least in part all the amazing things that you have given to me. The ripple effect of your influence continues through me onto others in my life. I hope you see the positive elements of the gifts you left in my care mirrored back to you through the success I've achieved in my career, the love I have for my family and my servant-leadership style. I am eternally grateful to you for sharing all that you had. THANK YOU!!!"

Julie Lupinacci is Hydro Ottawa's Chief Customer Officer. She administers programs/operations in furtherance of the company's 2016-2020 Strategic Direction, a five-year overview of business strategy and financial projections. This Strategic Direction sets out a balanced program for strong performance in existing operations, coupled with sustainable and profitable business growth. The strategy is customer-centric, financially responsible and responds to a strategic environment like increasing renewable generation capacity and enhancing customer value, operational effectiveness and Hydro Ottawa's contribution to the community.

CHAPTER 22

CONNIE MCINTYRE
Vice President of Customer Experience (Retired)
Southern Company Gas

Photo 22-1: Connie McIntyre

Any man who holds three jobs is a busy one, but the virtues I remember most about my dad were his humility and his ability to engage others with quiet effectiveness. That's probably why, in addition to owning a furniture store with my mom, her sister and his brother (yes, sisters married brothers and I was blessed with double first cousins!) and selling insurance, my dad was also a politician who served as a city council member and mayor for about 29 years in small town Jackson, Georgia. I always looked up to my dad. He taught me more by quiet example than with words. By watching his actions and unassuming, respectful manner with others, C. B. Brown planted his legacy in me and in Jackson. My brother Charlie Brown extended the Brown reputation when he later became mayor and served for 18 years. They are cut from the same cloth and both instilled great virtues in me. From the time I was old enough to

---

"Be vulnerable." – Connie McIntyre

---

understand, I realized my dad valued hard work and treating people well. When the town's constituents would call him about any nuisance or issue or gripe, my dad listened and responded. I guess that's why they kept electing him mayor. Those simple lessons were transferred to me, and now as I face my pending retirement from a company where I've worked for 40 years, I understand my own predilections: hard work, building relationships and producing results. After all, I am Mayor Brown's daughter.

As a young girl, I was a bit of a renegade and a little hardheaded. I liked to challenge rules and push boundaries much more than my older brother and sister even imagined. Having a mayor father should have curbed my independent streak, but that didn't stop me one afternoon from joining my classmates in a walk-out. That day, we'd learned our beloved football coach had been fired unexpectedly and without even asking us teenagers for our opinions. So, we town-kids left school without permission and walked back into town. Before cell phones, small town news ran faster than our adolescent legs walked. As we strode into town, my mother was waiting for me on the street in the family car. She unceremoniously put me in the passenger seat and promptly drove me back to school where an all-school assembly was being held to explain the situation. I was mortified that I had done something so rash that could embarrass my dad. On another occasion, I remember driving into town (with just my learner's permit) and seeing my dad chatting with the chief of police on the sidewalk. My dad later told me the chief pronounced, "Didn't know Connie was 16." To which, my dad replied, "I didn't know either." His opinions of me and the world around us shaped and defined my values. His lessons created the synapses and reactions that stayed with me quietly and reliably throughout my own long utility career.

A "big picture guy," Hank Linginfelter is a lot like my dad. The EVP of Southern Company Gas, Hank is skilled at hiring and promoting people with the right skills into

Photo 22-2: Me and my dad on my wedding day

Photo 22-3: My mentor Hank Linginfelter, a "big picture guy"

the right jobs. He is legendary at identifying people who were both knowl-edgeable in their field and demonstrated tried-and-true abilities to actually get things done. Very humble and patient, Hank calmed me down for years, especially with his signature phrase, "Major on the majors, Connie." I've worked with Hank for 33 years, and he promoted me to VP after I'd been at Southern Company for 30 years. Another of Hank's signature expressions, "Yearn to learn" meant to stretch to educate myself about other parts of the company. That's how Hank imprinted his "big picture" management philosophy, and he urged me to follow his footsteps. So, I did. I learned about operations and programs that stretched me beyond my office's walls and made me understand and appreciate the complex machinery of people, technology, processes, data, strategies and operational challenges that char-acterize today's gas utilities.

> "Major on the majors, but know the devil is in the detail."
> – Connie McIntyre

With Hank's support, we insourced calls sent to a call center in India back home to American shores, we integrated other companies acquired by SCG into its unique culture and practices, and we built a customer-centric culture throughout the organization, just to name a few accomplishments. Because of these efforts and the results produced, Southern Company Gas has won multiple J.D. Power and MSI awards for customer satisfaction and customer championship. Hank had my back from the beginning when I asked him to let me change my title from VP, Customer Service to VP, Customer Experience. Sometimes one word makes a difference. In this case, the one word "experience," was the touchstone to building a department that owned billing, remittance, credit and collections, voice of the customer and the call centers. By closely working with all the other departments, I was able to help everybody understand their role in the cus-tomer experience.

Catherine Land-Waters mentored me in powerful ways too. Catherine was the first female operations manager in our field operations, and she later became the VP of Customer Service and my boss. Catherine taught me to find and use my voice in the utility world. I remember vividly one of my first meetings with the senior leaders of our

Photo 22-4: Catherine Land-Waters, my mentor who taught me to have a voice

Photo 22-5: Bryan Batson, another key career mentor

company. I was quiet, and Catherine turned to me when we left, "Connie, no one knows as much as you do, and yet, you did not let them hear from you." I learned then to have a voice but one with humility and knowledge.

Another important mentor along the way was Bryan Batson. Now the president of several major companies, Bryan has a great sense of humor and treats everyone with respect. A good Christian man, Bryan keeps things simple. "Let it be all about them, Connie, not you. Just be good to people," he would say. Bryan taught me to just talk to people, anybody, everybody.

Rank and position, he believed, were secondary to letting people know that you cared about them, and not just their work and productivity, but also their family life, their personal successes and struggles away from the job and the challenges we all face along the journey called life. I learned from Bryan that I could be myself when I talked to employees, whether they were peers, subordinates or my bosses. He taught me that being vulnerable was human, not a crutch, and a trait that made me approachable and open to others.

"Realize the importance of living and playing and stopping to smell the roses along the way." – Connie McIntyre

---

So, if I could write a letter to the persons mentioned here, I'd start by remembering my dad's example and then listing the top 10 lessons learned:

- Listen to understand
- Respect others
- Be humble
- Be vulnerable
- Yearn to learn
- Maintain your integrity
- Connect the dots
- Know your audience
- Bloom where you are planted
- Major on the majors but know the devil is in the detail

My dad's example led me to people who taught important personal and career lessons and to places where I could achieve professionally. His example also girded me with resilience when personal struggles almost overtook me. My dad passed away shortly after I married my husband Bob. We were both young and vibrant and enjoyed being very active in life. When my husband was diagnosed with cancer and was sick off and on for the next 11 years, I relied on dear friendships to see me through. Along the way, my house burned down, and four years later I lost my husband; at times, the journey seemed more than I bargained for.

Today, as I look forward to spring 2018 and my upcoming retirement from Southern Company Gas, I have come to a place of peace. I've enjoyed a long and respected career, I have close and far-flung friends, and I realize the importance of living and playing and stopping to smell the roses along the way. One path is ending, but others are revealing themselves, and all is good. I leave in August 2018 to walk the Camino Santiago for 40 days. After all, I'm a bit headstrong and enjoy a walk brimming with purpose.

With operations in natural gas distribution, wholesale services, retail operations and midstream operations, Southern Company Gas (SCG) is one of the U.S.'s largest natural gas distribution companies. SCG cites four areas of its corporate social responsibility program: energy assistance, education, environmental stewardship and community enrichment. Before her February 2018 retirement as SCG's Vice President of Customer Experience, Connie McIntyre led the utility's CIS replacement project as its executive sponsor. In a new role, McIntyre takes the reins as CS Week's Executive Summit venue executive with CS Week 2019 in Phoenix.

CHAPTER 23

PENNI MCLEAN-CONNER
Chief Customer Officer and SVP of Customer Care
Eversource

Photo 23-1: Penni McLean-Conner

Name a mentor(s) that taught you key lessons at a young age. Describe those lessons. John and Cathy McLean. I grew up in Horse Shoe, North Carolina, just off a dirt road, on a large dairy farm. My Mom and Dad, John and Cathy McLean, were my biggest champions, coaches and mentors. They instilled in me early on that you can't just have ideas or dreams, you must share them. And you can't just speak, you must 'speak up.'

And learn to 'speak up' is what my Mom and Dad coached me in so well in our local 4-H club. They coached me in speaking the way many parents today might coach their kids in soccer or hockey.

My first public speaking opportunity was at the county 4-H competition. I was 8 years old, and I proudly presented on the appropriate technique of giving calves shots using a calf plushy that my Mom had made. I practiced my presentation with my Dad, who would remind me to slow down and not

---

"I must be true to myself." – Penni McLean-Conner

---

say 'uh.' The hours of practice paid off, and I was successful not only at the county level, but also at the district level, leading to the state finals.

Today, I must speak up often in personal and professional situations. Because of the years of practice, I am comfortable speaking up in small settings or at large venues. Most importantly by speaking up, I gained confidence and with confidence, collaboration and leadership. Their early guidance has carried me throughout my academic and professional career.

"You can't just have ideas or dreams, you must share them. And you can't just speak, you must 'speak up.'"
– Penni McLean-Conner

Name a mentor that taught you key lessons in your business career. Describe those lessons. Sharon Decker. My passion for and understanding of the business of utility customer service was largely developed during my tenure at Duke Power's customer service center. I had the opportunity to work for Duke Power's first female vice president, Sharon Decker, to support the establishment of a centralized 24/7 customer service center in the early 1990s.

Sharon was an amazing mentor. She led Duke Power's transition from face-to-face customer service at nearly 100 business offices to a 24/7 call center that offered customers self-service. While more commonplace today, the offering of 24-hour customer services became a model for the utility industry.

I learned many lessons from Sharon, but most importantly, I learned how to demonstrate care and empathy for employees. Sharon did this by personally connecting with employees, recognizing employees for their accomplishments and sharing stories. Sharon knew every employee, not only their names, but importantly their goals. She encouraged and supported employees in small group settings, in one-on-ones and by constantly walking the call center floor. She recognized employees with awards, celebrations and via emails and the call center newsletter. And she used stories to explain business concepts. Sharon shared stories of success, challenges and business goals to align the entire call center team around their mission to provide great service.

Sharon Decker helped me understand that to provide great care to customers, you first must provide great care to employees. I use her lessons daily as I work to enable our Eversource team to provide great care and service to our customers.

Describe key lessons that may have been well-intentioned by mentors but rightfully fell into the category of "Please Don't Emulate." Merriam Webster defines emulate as 'to strive to equal.' While I do study leaders with characteristics that I admire, I have learned that I will fail in trying to 'equal' them. What I mean is that while I do study leaders habits and work methods, I do not try to become them. Rather, I work to adapt their work methods into my style.

Over my career, I have tried to emulate leaders without success, for example, Nick Conner, a consultant for teams and leaders, and my husband. In fact, I met Nick when he worked with my leadership team at Tampa Electric. The two days we spent together as a team completing experiential learning exercises designed by Nick, fast-forwarded our development as a team and propelled our success in transforming our service.

Nick is a fantastic facilitator and consultant. I wanted to be like him, so I jumped at the chance to join him on a large team-building program, leading experiential exercises, and importantly facilitating the learnings from these exercises. Nick trained me, and I was positive that I could 'emulate' him as a facilitator.

But I am not Nick. I was not particularly good at facilitating the exercises and discussion. It was not natural to me and caused me to be both nervous and anxious.

My take-away from this experience is that I must be true to myself. As previously noted in describing Sharon Decker, I worked to identify her actions that demonstrated caring, then adapting them to my leadership style.

"She used stories to explain business concepts… stories of success, challenges, and business goals to align the entire call center team around their mission to provide great service." – Penni McLean-Conner

---

If you could write a letter to the mentors in #1, #2 or #3 above, what would you say?

Dear Sharon,

Thank you for your inspiration and leadership. Your career both in private and public service has touched so many. I am proud that I had the opportunity to work with you early in my career at Duke Power.

Employees would walk on water for you, because they knew you truly cared about each of them. From you, I learned not only the importance of caring for each employee and how this translated to amazing care for customers, but I learned important techniques in how to demonstrate that care for employees.

You are also an inspiration. Your career is noteworthy, from being named the first woman and youngest vice president at Duke Power to your most recent role as North Carolina's Secretary of Commerce. And, you are proudly a mom of four. I watched closely how you managed both your personal and professional life.

I wish you continued success. Thank you for your advice, leadership and inspiration.

Sincerely,
Penni

Likewise a CS Week Publishing author with her 2017 hit, *Profiles in Excellence: Utility Chief Customer Officers*, Penni McLean-Conner serves as Chief Customer Officer and SVP of Customer Care at Eversource, an electric, natural gas and water services company headquartered in Hartford, CT and Boston, MA. In 2012, Northeast Utilities and four of its operating companies merged with NSTAR Electric & Gas, paving the way for the creation of Eversource Energy in 2015. Eversource acquired Aquarion Water Company in December 2017, making it the only US electric company that also owns a water company. These mergers and acquisitions make the Eversource customer base nearly 4 million strong.

CHAPTER 24

CECIL MCMASTER
Chief Information Officer
New York City Department of Environmental Protection

Photo 24-1: Cecil McMaster

My first mentor was my mom, Cecille Fleming McMaster. Her number one job was taking care of the family. She was committed to us, her five kids and dad. She taught me a very important lesson at a young age about commitment and caring. She made many sacrifices for us, she guided us as young kids with her words of wisdom, she made sure we went to school, she made sure we studied at night, she always said, "Be the best you can be all the time." So, like my mom committed years to me and our family, I commit to my teams today. I care intensely about their well-being, I want them to be successful with their jobs and lives. I want them to have successful careers. When you care for your teams, they know it, and you get the best out of

---

Remember to schedule time off, take vacations and refresh
from time to time. – Cecil McMaster

---

them. When the teams are the best they can be, the customers in the end benefits tremendously. Happy teams, happy customers.

I worked in the financial industry in the late 1990s as a systems engineer with Randy Crannin. Randy was my manager for the first few years. I learned from him early on that I needed to focus on improving my communication skills. I needed to understand that a huge part of communicating was listening carefully to what was being said or asked of our team. It is so easy to get carried away with all the technology floating around us and so easy to miss what our customers' needs are. I stress to my teams every chance I get to make sure we communicate and listen to other team members and our customers. Another lesson I learned over the years was to do the work, put the time in, keep learning all the time because things are changing so fast. The more you know the more valuable you are to the company and customers.

> "When you care for your teams, they know it, and you get the best out of them. When the teams are the best they can be, the customers in the end benefits tremendously. Happy teams, happy customers." – Cecil McMaster

One aspect that I crossed in my career and have being trying to leave behind is being too serious about work all the time. Work must be fun, we must enjoy what we do, and we must do what we like for work. I was hired some years ago as a programmer by Mike Sasko, whom I worked for about three years at NYC DEP. Mike always presented our team back then with challenges, but he always guided us, working closely with the team, asking questions to get us to think creatively to solve problems. We worked hard and long hours for many years, we loved what we did and we had fun most of the time. Mike was always encouraging and positive and had a "we can do it" attitude no matter what. When we enjoy the work we do, we do our best work. When we do our best work, everyone benefits. Remember to take time off, vacations and get refreshed from time to time.

> Listen carefully to what is being said or asked of your team. It is so easy to get carried away with all the technology floating around us and so easy to miss what our customers' needs are. – Cecil McMaster

If I could reach back in time with a letter addressed to these significant influencers, it would say:

Dear Mentors:

Thank you for being there all those years. The wisdom you imparted on me will never be forgotten. Your guidance and advice were always valued. I did not always appreciate all that was taught the first time, but in time it all made sense. I must tell you, to be a great leader you must care about the people and teams who work with you. Most importantly, I learned over the years from all of you that you cared about the people and teams. You were vested in their success.

Thank you, Mom, Randy and Mike

The New York City Department of Environmental Protection (DEP) is a municipal agency of nearly 6,000 employees that manages and conserves the city's water supply; distributes clean drinking water and collects wastewater for nine million New Yorkers; and treats wastewater in a way that protects the quality of New York Harbor. Cecil McMaster is New York City DEP's Chief Information Officer. He has over 15 years' experience delivering technology solutions and services to automate and support this utility's business processes.

CHAPTER 25

KERRY OVERTON
Deputy General Manager and Chief Customer Officer
Austin Energy

Photo 25-1: Kerry Overton

Encouragement, support, positivism: that's the bottom line for the mentors who shaped my life and outlook. Let me introduce a few whose influences were early, long and impactful.

An obituary may seem an odd place to begin reminiscing about my mentors, but this one strikes a personal chord and provides the background and roadmap for the story I want to tell. Written upon the death of my dad, Hardy Overton, Sr. in 2012, it sums up so many lessons he and others taught me:

"...After high school graduation, he entered the U.S. Air Force on August 13, 1952, proudly serving as a Staff Sergeant (SSGT) and fire fighter for over twenty years....

"Ordained as a deacon, Hardy, Sr. grew to love his church and enjoyed serving others. When Reverend Obey passed away, Hardy, Sr. embraced a new pastor, the beloved Reverend Joseph C. Parker, Jr. Under Pastor Parker's leadership Deacon Overton was involved in the Platinum Plus Senior Adult Ministry, the Men's Ministry, the Outreach Ministry, and as Coordinator of Wednesday Noon Bible Study. Additionally, he dutifully

Photo 25-2: Hardy Overton, Sr., my dad

Photo 25-3: My mother, Betty Overton

served as Chairman of David Chapel's Finance Committee and received 'Man of the Year' recognition in 2005.

"The Christian principles Deacon Overton strived to achieve in his ministry were the same ones he instilled in his family. As a proud and supportive father, through love and discipline, he taught his children the value of hard work and service, respect for others, responsibility, confidence and unity…"[1]

As for my mom… she is the nicest person I know. Really. Her pleasant demeanor is a trait everyone loves about her. She tries to solve problems without much dissention while maintaining respect for everyone involved. She doesn't shy away from conflict. Instead, she goes to great lengths to ensure people's well-being and spirits are taken care of in a positive way. During my childhood, she was a stay-at-home mom for a time, but she also worked as a nurse serving underprivileged kids and mentally and emotionally challenged adults in what was then called the Texas Department of Mental Health and Mental Retardation.

Like most, my stories about mentors and the lessons they taught begin with my father and mother, Hardy and Betty Overton. After reading the obituary clip above, you probably won't be surprised when I share that my dad was a strong person both physically and mentally. Together, my dad and mom inspired each of their six children (including me, their youngest). They led with their faith in Jesus Christ as their savior. They modeled a sense of duty, a respect for community and a graciousness for the church. My dad provided structure and continuity and shared a sincere commitment to helping others. Growing up with a father like Hardy Overton, Sr. and a mother like Betty Overton was grounding, even when our family struggled at times to make ends meet. Together, my parents worked hard, they treated people well, and they reached success on the principle that there's more that all of us can achieve together rather than trying to work through life by eliminating or oppressing and suppressing others.

---

1   http://www.fuller-sheffieldfuneral.com/

These are snapshots of the parents who raised me. The values they instilled at home with me and my brothers and sisters became the foundation for my academic, athletic, personal and career success. The basics were all there: work hard, take responsibility for your actions and words and the way they influence others, stay positive, be encouraging and support people whenever and wherever. Those values were imprinted on me in school, on and off the playing fields, and they inform and guide me today in the corporate suite.

Try to solve problems without much dissention while maintaining respect for everyone involved. Don't shy away from conflict. Instead, go to great lengths to ensure people's well-being and spirits are taken care of in a positive way. – Kerry Overton

---

Other mentors echoed their lessons. Teachers throughout my school and college years valued diversity and really encouraged me. Jim Davis was one of those. As my high school football coach in 1978-82 at LBJ High School in Austin, Texas, where Jaguar football has a long and proud history, Coach Davis really enjoyed being around great student athletes. He pushed me and my teammates to the highest level of gridiron success based on two cornerstones: responsibility and consistency. We didn't just talk about it; we put it to work. By maintaining a regular routine and being prepared, he taught us that mental and physical readiness allowed us to execute and rise to the challenge. As the quarterback, I enjoyed more interaction with him because of my position. During one memorable game against a rival team, we faced a very taxing moment when a sense of fear and doubt began creeping into the team. As Coach Davis and I were communicating about potential plays and their execution, he emphasized, "You are the leader." Instinctively knowing his next unspoken words, I realized I had to be one of those leaders who changed doubt into determination. It was my job to prove up the promise that if we believed in our plan, we could execute it together. "You're here, you've done this before. You've led this team, and you've got to do what you do," Coach urged. While I wasn't the only player on the field, I was their leader, and it was my duty to lead confidently. It was the tough situations that brought out the natural competitive nature in me. It was in these situations that I learned more about doing your best, competing to win and doing so with a moral compass.

As I transitioned to my early career, John Hall was another mentor who shared powerful lessons. At the time we worked together, John was the

Deputy Commissioner of the Energy Resources Department at the Texas General Land Office, led by Commissioner Garry Mauro. John hired me as one of his executive assistants in policy and energy resource management. Knowing my strong academic and athletic background from four years at Rice University, John was comfortable piling on the work. Yes, it was a lot of responsibility early in my career, but he knew that with my strong work ethic, I would deliver. I won his trust, and together we accomplished a lot. "Think it through," John would say, meaning that I needed to look at the big picture, engage others in tackling multiple tasks and pay attention to the details. His advice also meant I should approach assignments from a broader policy perspective because other stakeholders could be impacted. Working under that situation was like drinking from a firehose because I was tasked with large, complex assignments, but John taught me to develop a schematic in my mind, look for what-if scenarios and plan for contingencies. He helped me develop a foundational way of thinking and, as I gained experience, it became second nature for me. We worked together for five years and remain in contact, particularly at community events, where we revisit fond memories from our Land Office days.

> Be one of those leaders who changes doubt into determination. Prove up the promise that if we believe in our plan, we can execute it together. – Kerry Overton

---

While John taught me sound research, development and decision-making processes, Garry pushed me even more. I was promoted to Deputy Commissioner after several job assignments at the Texas General Land Office. While my training and natural tendencies (as an oil and gas auditor) led me to approach work in a calculated manner, Garry gave me his confidence to take risks, especially when dealing with unknown variables in program development as an emerging leader. Men of integrity both, John and Garry nurtured and enabled me to set sound policy (and industry practices) for multiple stakeholders and then expand/modify/adjust those policy perimeters when situations or business objectives demanded.

This background equipped me for my current role as Deputy General Manager and Chief Customer Office at Austin Energy. I very much enjoy the work I do for a public utility on behalf of our customers. In my role, I have responsibilities to our client departments, and it's common to have multiple stakeholders whose interests align, but it's more often the case that stakeholder priorities conflict. My job is to solve these problems. By demonstrating accountability to individuals and meeting their customized needs, I serve as a great steward of the larger resources and help others in the program services we provide based on varying needs of the community.

Photo 25-4: My pastor, the Reverend Joseph C. Parker, Jr.

My father's obituary mentioned Joseph C. Parker, Jr., my beloved pastor and a man who knows my history since I was a young man. Throughout my life, Pastor Parker has modeled his own spiritual development and helped me grow mine. He is a man of tremendous personal faith tempered by humor. With my natural tendencies towards seriousness, Pastor Parker helps me stay balanced, so I can see the weighty and the important as well as the silly, the absurd and the down-right funny.

Growing up as an African-American young man, I heard a lot of people make connections between athletic success and business success. People would tell me, "You have to be twice as good as everybody else." That advice never rang true for me. Instead, I like to think we have to muster the courage to believe in ourselves and be the best we each can be. In my ball-playing years, one day I realized the math: If you're only given 20 attempts to throw the ball, you can't throw 40 completions. Well-intentioned as the advice about being doubly good may be, I'm not buying it, and I don't share that advice with my son or others I mentor. Rather, I encourage them to understand who they are and start with the confidence that who they are is good enough. Then, the additional development work builds the person up to achieve more by setting goals and working their plan. With determination, hard work, encouragement and support, the possibilities are great. I believe in accepting people for who they are and starting from that place of their own significance, not placing conditions and thinking they must be twice as good to succeed.

Develop a schematic in your mind, look for what-if scenarios and plan for contingencies. – Kerry Overton

My life and the lessons I've learned reflect so many people who have invested in me, encouraged me, been positive and stayed supportive. I make no apologies for the contributions that athletics have made in my life. Playing on a team helped me find balance, set goals, compete when the stakes were high and know the real measure of what I put into a challenge directly influenced the outcome and what I got out of it. Those shared experiences of success and winning are memories no one can erase, and the bonds forged between teammates and coaches are unbreakable.

I remain humble. My wife and collective family keep me on that keel. And my mom inspires me to be nice and fair. Forging forward, making tough decision, taking risks even when dealing with some unknowns, operating with others' interest in mind; it's all about the work and the effort I put into it. And more importantly, it's the people I value and appreciate. I know because my mentors have so valued and supported me.

> The eighth largest, publicly-owned US electric utility, Austin Energy successfully fulfills its mission to safely deliver clean, affordable, reliable energy and excellent customer service. With nearly 450,000 customers and a service population of almost a million, this electric service provider was recently named the 2018 Smart Energy Power Alliance's Public Power Utility of the Year. This honor speaks to the investment and commitment Austin Energy has made in transitioning to a clean, modern energy future. Austin Energy is a customer-driven and community-focused organization committed to business excellence. Kerry Overton is Austin Energy's Deputy General Manager and Chief Customer Officer.

CHAPTER 26

ANDREA PELT-THORNTON
IT Agile Manager
NextEra Energy, Inc./Florida Power & Light Company

Photo 26-1: Andrea Pelt-Thornton

One mentor who taught me one of my most fundamental lessons is Mrs. Sarah Cherry, my fourth-grade teacher. Much like the saying, "Everything I needed to know, I learned in kindergarten," Mrs. Cherry's lessons were everything I needed to know to survive and thrive. You see, Mrs. Cherry taught me, a smart but shy student who skipped the third grade, that any disadvantage that I'd ever perceive to have was irrelevant. Even though the other students were bigger than me, my size was irrelevant, so I had to stand up for myself and participate. Even though I missed the third-grade lessons in fractions, it was irrelevant. Crying wasn't an option; I had to be a big girl who learned fast and let my little light shine.

Additionally, my parents, Willie and Johnnie Pelt, were my first teachers.

"Stand up, avoid self-pity and be confident, even in intimidating circumstances." – Andrea Pelt-Thornton

They gave me life's greatest lesson – to believe that I could achieve anything that I set my mind to do.

Stick to your principles and be forthright with business partners, even when they might not like what you have to say. – Andrea Pelt-Thornton

---

In the end, those lessons to stand up, avoid self-pity and be confident, even in intimidating circumstances, were fundamental to my personal growth and success.

There were several mentors who taught by example key lessons in my business career. Gene Smith (former Director of Distribution), Bill Hamilton (VP of Customer Service, retired) and Dennis Klinger (CIO, retired) taught me the importance of standing by your word and standing by your team members, as they are keys to success. While implementing a new Customer Information System, there were many controversial decisions and trade-offs that had to be made. These colleagues demonstrated the importance of sticking to your principles and being forthright with business partners, even when they might not like what you have to say. In the end, you will be respected for treating people with respect, being honest and being committed to doing the right thing.

Another business colleague, Yvonne Squire, one of the first African American team leaders in IT development, taught me it was okay to speak softly but be a heavy weight by knowing your stuff. She reiterated Mrs. Cherry's lesson to not be intimidated, even though you are one-of-a-kind, in a very male-dominated industry.

"It was okay to speak softly but be a heavy weight by knowing your stuff." – Andrea Pelt-Thornton

---

Dear friends, thank you for shaping me into the person that I am today. You were watched and were more impactful to me than you could ever know.

The third largest electric utility in the United States and a subsidiary of NextEra Energy, Florida Power & Light Company serves an estimated 10 million people across nearly half of the state of Florida. The company received the top ranking in the southern U.S. among large electric providers, according to the J.D. Power 2016 Electric Utility Residential Customer Satisfaction Study (SM). In her position as IT Agile Manager, Andrea Pelt-Thornton has helped implement many strategic systems and enabling applications that form the building blocks of the FPL customer experience.

CHAPTER 27

BECKY POPE
IT Applications Manager
Greenville Utilities Commission

Photo 27-1: Becky Pope

First of all, I don't like the names, "boss," "manager" or "supervisor." I prefer the name or term, "leader." I believe good leaders follow their heart, their gut, history, and they utilize different philosophies or styles, depending upon the situation and the team member. No style or philosophy is right or wrong. Vince Lombardi once said, "It's not how many times you get knocked down; it's how many times you get back up." Sometimes, it may take multiple tries to reach a team member or coach a high performing team, but true leaders give their all.

I started thinking about this the other day when I was asked how many years I have been a manager and a leader. I'm 58 years old, and I responded with the answer, 55 years. I've been reading letters from my hard-working father while he was in Vietnam, and in quite a few of those letters, he referenced me as a leader. I enjoy team environments and was always wondering how I could convince people to do certain things. I think good leaders have certain personality traits, but I also believe some of it is learning, patience, passion and desire.

> "I believe good leaders follow their heart, their gut, history, and they utilize different philosophies or styles, depending upon the situation and the team member. No style or philosophy is right or wrong." – Becky Pope

Over the many years of my career, I have had opportunities to listen to great leaders and have been enriched with leadership classes of various styles. One of my favorite, and I think greatest, leaders is Vince Lombardi. I recommend reading his thought-provoking quotes even though they are related to football teams. While reading them, think of the team that you are leading or supervising. Vince Lombardi once said, "Coaches who can outline plays on a black board are a dime a dozen. The ones who win get inside their player and motivate."

I truly believe that managers who manage from their office or project plan have less effective teams than those who get in the trenches and work with their team. I call this "boots on the ground leadership." In my previous years, I have had the opportunity to work for both types; notice I said, "Worked, not lead." The managers who were buried in their offices or in the project plans could not relate to those on the project nor could they understand the true duration of a task. As they say, "The devil is in the details." Don't get me wrong, I believe in task lists, target dates and plans, but there is also reality. Believe it or not, I am thankful I had some miserable experiences. It showed me how not to lead an effective team and keep morale going in tough times.

> "Even after good communications, to keep a good relationship intact, it is best to present and move on when sometimes you don't agree." – Becky Pope

In the early years of my career, the management style was not team oriented. It was a "do as I say" type management. There was not any investment in the individual or communication. What I felt was good for the company usually contradicted the manager's direction. Due to my desire and love of being a leader, I persevered by seeking support from others with similar leadership style and beliefs, knowing in my heart that one day an opening within the company would present itself for me to fulfill my dream. After approximately two years, I had my break to lead a small team and fulfill my goal of doing what was best for the company, even though at times I did not make friends along the way.

Photo 27-2: George Reel, my mentor and GUC's Director of Customer Relations

Over time, I have been through many adventures which provided me positive opportunities, thanks to two exceptional leaders. First, there was George Reel, Director of Customer Relations. He mentored me and provided personal encouragement to continue fighting for my beliefs even though I never reported directly to him. George taught me that at times people just want someone to listen. He helped me learn about the relationships which needed to be built for a solid team foundation. He taught me that people need to know they are cared about and that the company and its customers are always priorities.

Photo 27-3: Me and Sandy Barnes, GUC's Director of Information Technology

The last fifteen years, I worked for Sandy Barnes, Director of Information Technology. She has invested a priceless amount of time, both personal and professional, in me and my team. Her investment is not just training, but boots on the ground, getting down in the trenches. There is always an open-door policy, 100% honesty, trust and best intentions for the people with Sandy. We have a relationship that we can vent and agree to disagree, but we work together to come up with a solution. Our common end goal is our company, customer service and a high performing team.

I have learned through the years that it is okay to be the boss. What is important is your treatment of the team members and believing and investing in people, while supporting and working with them. Many in my field are analytic, independent thinkers who like challenges. It is critical to provide and support an effective environment instead of squashing their thought processes by making them doers. Analytic, independent thinkers become ineffective if a leader does not use their strengths and empower them to make decisions.

Another lesson learned is that it is okay to not know everything in detail. Getting back to people with information is fine but be sure to do so in a timely manner. Good leaders have a strong team they support and trust. Depending on the team's responsibilities, having all the details may not be possible, so empower the team to respond and communicate.

A previous general manager and my current leader use the old proverb, "Good fences make good neighbors." Effective communication by leaders at all levels in the organization is very important for success. The message needs to be clear and definitive. The ability to ensure expectations and decisions made are understood will help reinforce good relationships. Finding the proper words can be very difficult at times. However, having documentation and open lines of communication allow each party to understand each other.

Practice "boots on the ground" leadership. Get in the trenches and work with your team. – Becky Pope

---

Even after good communications, to keep a good relationship intact, it is best to present and move on when sometimes you don't agree. Whether it is timing, policies, chain of command, politics or any other factor, there are occasions when diplomatic presentation of the case and waiting are the best actions. This posture is extremely hard to maintain when passions are high or the result of the decision will be an anticipated failure. If another opportunity presents itself, be prepared with a rescue or alternative plan.

Through years of good leadership, I have learned those who get in the trenches truly understand and will have a high chance of enjoying an effective team. Getting to know each member as a person to help them become an effective employee builds the trust and respect needed to be "the boss." Those on the front line or in the trenches know 100% of the problems. As one works his or her way up the organizational chart, these problems become lesser known, which hurts the organization. Sure, upper management deals with tough problems of a different nature; however, the front line is the company's base. Organizations that run with leaders who have low-performing or mediocre-performing team members will eventually fall apart in retention, customer service and overall performance.

All of these qualities were taught to me through career opportunities and exposure to all levels of an organization. Unfortunately, I am nearing an end to my time with the best leaders I have had during my employment. Soon, they will be moving on to next chapters in life like retirement. I will still be a successful, effective leader by following their teachings and learning from opportunities and challenges. As I quoted Vince Lombardi earlier, his wise words strengthen my resolve. Many thanks to my mentors for their belief in me and their priceless mentoring. Like Lombardi knew, true leaders, like me, have the confidence and the tools to get back up.

Greenville Utilities Commission provides electric, water, sewer and natural gas services to about 150,000 customers living in the City of Greenville and 75% of Pitt County in North Carolina. Its mission emphasizes enhancing the quality of life by safely providing reliable utility solutions at the lowest reasonable cost, with exceptional customer service in an environmentally responsible manner. Becky Pope, an IT Applications Manager at Greenville Utilities, served for eight years as an active member on the CS Week Planning Committee and was the project manager of GUC's recent Customer Information System implementation project team.

CHAPTER 28

HALLIE REESE
VP & Chief Customer Officer
Exelon Utilities

Photo 28-1: Hallie Reese

To borrow and turn a phrase, "Almost everything I need to know I learned on the softball field." Credits and apologies but revising the title of Robert Fulghum's best-seller helps share stories about my childhood mentor. Lee Chappine was my high school softball coach. His skills and ability to win at the highest level of competition attracted the very best players with a lot of talent. I was his premiere pitcher in the early 1980s. We were not your normal high school team; in my last two years in high school, we lost just three games and won over 50, including the first ever state championship in the history of the school. Other teams considered us a dynasty because Coach Chappine's success was assured and legendary. I reached the pinnacle of high school athletic success as the first female windmill softball pitcher in southern New Jersey.

Three foundational lessons from Coach Chappine's playbook served me well then and have carried me forward to the C-Suite and throughout personal situations as well.

Photo 28-2: Lee Chappine, my high school softball coach

1.   There is absolutely no substitution for paying attention to the details.

Lee was a stickler about the little things. The way we wore our uniforms, the way we acted on the field, the way we studied opponents and the way we practiced. From being around him, I began to understand how important the little things are – they add up! Being focused on things that most people ignore creates a mindset which allows you to excel. You know, with certainty, that you have done all you can do to ensure the right outcome. And for those situations where you do not succeed, you can rest assured that you gave it all you had. It wasn't some little 'thing' that tripped you up.

2.   Anticipate situations you will encounter and prepare to face them.

As part of our practice routine, Lee would put us into very difficult game situations and have us work out of them time and time again. Squeeze bunts, double tandem cutoffs on balls hit into the outfield gaps – you name it, we practiced it. Consequently, we knew how to handle anything other teams could dish out because we practiced every option or permutation imaginable. Lee taught me to consider and prepare for the "what ifs," and I have applied this learning many times in my personal and professional life. Since I am now conditioned to think about "what ifs," I feel that I am better prepared to react when something does happen.

3.   It's okay to admit when you're wrong.

I almost missed Lee's invaluable lessons. As a gifted eighth grade softball player, my dad started me pitching. At the tender age of 14, I was a bit of a hothead, and Lee made an off-handed comment to the effect of, "She will never play for me," within earshot of a family member. His words stuck in my craw. I deserved his criticism, but I was bound and determined to prove him wrong. I couldn't allow this person who didn't really know me to dictate my outcomes. So, I listened well and accepted his guidance and criticism; I practiced and then practiced some more. Many years later, Lee and I shared an adult conversation about his judgmental comment and our journey together as coach/player. He admitted that his comments were rough and had he known what type of worker I was, he most likely would not have made them. Walking away from that experience, I learned that as a leader, I must always keep my mind open about the talent around me. I have to work to understand who they are and particularly how to motivate their various talents. In my case, it was incredibly empowering to recognize that Lee had misjudged me. In that discussion, I realized that it's not so much about how great someone's talent is. It's more about that you have to look at where they are, appreciate their strengths, not dismiss them too quickly and recognize how to motivate them.

Photo 28-3: Family photo with my grandfather, Dan Salerno

Another mentor was closer to home. Dan Salerno, my grandfather, was a first generation American. His parents immigrated from Italy to the Philadelphia area for a better life and didn't speak English. Times being what they were, it was tough on Italian immigrants. That first generation born thereafter would have it easier because of their parents' determination against hard times. My grandfather was a very smart, self-made man. With just a middle school education, he worked at Nabisco Company, taking the train to Philadelphia every workday. He was always reaching for something bigger and better for himself. His wife worked in a sewing factory, and eventually they ended up buying the factory with another partner. They ran it for years. In retirement, he owned three homes and several rental properties. I was lucky enough to have him in my life into my late 20s before he died. I remember him teaching me and his other grandchildren to be a person of your word. "Don't lie," he'd caution. "Don't manufacture the truth. It's only your word and your integrity that you have at the end of the day."

Carrying his wise words with me as I started working in the utility industry in the 1990s, I've been blessed with diverse experiences and fortunate to have run several critical, high-profile projects for the C-Suite. My colleagues understood that I was going to pay attention to the little things. I was always prepared because I'd thought through the options, their benefits and their consequences. Executives who trusted me to run these projects appreciated that I'd give an honest assessment to tough questions and never tell them what I thought they wanted to hear. Lessons learned from Lee Chappine and Dan Salerno are deeply engrained in who I am today.

"There is absolutely no substitution for paying attention to the details." – Hallie Reese

---

Atlantic City Electric Company's Chief Financial Officer Mike Barron became an important mentor in my early utility days. Back in 1996, I was serving in an acting role as the lead executive for internal audit. Here I was a 36-year-old woman in an industry dominated by seasoned men. In the six years I'd worked for Atlantic City Electric, I'd gone from being the junior auditor to the youngest executive in the company. I interviewed for the permanent position with many others, and when Mike offered me the job, he said, "Hallie, reach high and think big." What a blockbuster moment to have a C-level executive think enough of me to say those empowering words! It gave me the go-ahead to think differently about the position's functions, to engage with my team and figure out how we would operate in potentially different ways, to push myself past the status quo. It also granted me space and latitude to stretch myself around my capabilities. I had witnessed first-hand how Mike lived that principle and ran this team. He never took situations at face value, but asked good, probing questions. He taught me to lead others with this methodology. I've learned that I don't need to have all the answers and tell people what to do; instead, by asking questions and letting them answer, they usually figure out what needs to happen and what steps to take. By affirming their opinions and teaching them to solve they own problems, I show them their value and their potential. Sure, we exchange questions and answers, banter options and consider alternatives. These activities guide them to the right recommendations. We are more productive as a team, and I sure learn a lot more by asking questions instead of delivering instructions.

Another mentor who dropped a simple phrase on me one day that burrowed into my brain and became a pearl of wisdom was Marilyn Powell, Senior Vice President of Marketing at Atlantic City Electric. She told me, "Pick a mood." Three simple words, but they are so powerful and so empowering. She explained that every day, each of us can get up and pick any mood we want to be in; you are in control of your mood. On the days when I'm sick of riding trains or flying in planes because of my travel schedule, I recall Marilyn's pearl. I can pick a mood because today is new, it's not yesterday and it's not tomorrow. It's today, and I get the opportunity to interact as I choose – I pick to be curious or energetic or happy or something else. The subtle power of this phrase is that I don't let the events of the day overtake me. Engaging with this phrase every day creates a very productive, positive and intentional frame of mind. I can pick a mood of fear or a mood of "Hey, this is great, I get to interact." It allows me to enter a room or a conversation with a very intentional mindset, so I don't allow others or bad news to highjack me.

"'Don't lie,' he'd caution. 'Don't manufacture the truth. It's only your word and your integrity that you have at the end of the day.'" – Hallie Reese

---

"Pick a mood" also taught me to take one day at a time. Since 1996, I've been through three utility mergers, and along the way there's been a lot of relearning, new people and different processes. I've held 13 positions since 2001 throughout those mergers in addition to those critical projects mentioned earlier. Marilyn's tip has served me well as I learned new leadership teams, understood new company cultures, worked with different people, lost and gained institutional knowledge, re-honed credibility and navigated more ambiguity and uncertainty than most. But when I pick a mood, I am empowered to stay focused, prepared and ready to tackle the next challenge.

Along the way, I also witnessed a powerful lesson that taught me, "Don't follow that example." I hold great respect for this person, but his old-school methodologies and overly protective nature caused him to become the target of a ruinous reorganization of his team. He had built an organization that was perceived as strident and inflexible. He held others at arm's length, making sure everyone knew that his turf was solid, and suggestions were unnecessary and unwelcome. He was one of those who didn't want anybody in his swim lane. He surrounded himself with like-minded sycophants who imitated these attitudes. So, when a massive reorg was announced, fellow executives decapitated his organization with a gusto. It turned out horrifically for his people. Every one of his staff was dismissed or moved to other responsibilities. What did I learn from his disastrous example? I learned that to gain power you have to give up power. As an executive, I can say, "This is my organization and I don't want you looking at it or making suggestions." But to influence my peers, I can't think that way, especially if it's a function that enables others. I learned that by inviting others to tell me things about my organization, I have more credibility by demonstrating that I'm not a turf protector. I have learned through all the mergers that all power shifts and wanes, ebbs and flows to others in the organization. By listening, helping others succeed and sharing power, I become more resilient and my organizations less susceptible to being torn down by others. By taking down the wall a little at a time and letting others look into and influence my organization, I've learned that 'jack-of-all-trades' and 'team player' are great nicknames I'm proud to be called.

"She told me, 'Pick a mood.' Three simple words, but they are so powerful and so empowering. She explained that every day, each of us can get up and pick any mood we want to be in; you are in control of your mood."
– Hallie Reese

When I think about my important mentors, there is one thing they all have in common: they all understood that as a leader you cast a very long shadow. The conversations you have with people, the things you choose to say or not, the behaviors you choose to demonstrate or not: everyone is watching. I've learned I have to be "on" every day because that's the responsibility I shoulder as a leader. The lessons and truths my mentors shared were informal at the moment they were delivered. I didn't even think to write them down. But the casual became impactful once I internalized their meaning and reflected on the opportunities. These lessons traverse my life – they apply at work, in how I treat friends and family, how I've raised children and now, as roles are reversing, how I'm becoming my mother's caretaker. I don't always get it right, but I'm very mindful of the shadow I cast because of these incredible teachers.

A Fortune 100 behemoth, Exelon Corporation is the largest US electric parent company, with approximately 10 million customers served by 34,000 employees. Created in October 2000 with the merger of PECO Energy Company (Philadelphia) and Unicom Corp, the owner of Commonwealth Edison (Chicago), its eight operating subsidiaries include: Exelon Generation, Constellation Energy Group and six regulated utilities, Commonwealth Edison, PECO Energy Company, Baltimore Gas and Electric, Delmarva Power & Light, Atlantic City Electric and Potomac Electric Power Company. In her role as VP and Chief Customer Officer, Hallie Reese is responsible for implementing customer experience strategies across the regulated utilities.

CHAPTER 29

KIM RICH
Customer Solutions Manager
CenterPoint Energy

Photo 29-1: Kim Rich

They were strength for me. My grandmothers, Carolyn Allen, Audrey Brock and Grace Lindsey influenced me from a very early age, embracing our 'grand' relationship and teaching me the uniqueness of each individual's personality, skills, tastes and foibles. As the oldest granddaughter, I was blessed to enjoy their attentions and lessons for the longest time. I treasure those memories, summer road trips, holiday traditions and one vivid spring break where instead of a beach trip I chose a memory-filled March week with just me and my grandmas riding the Amtrak from East Texas to Chicago. Our easy conversations, the laughter, frequent winks and hugs; our trip was remarkable not for what we visited or saw but for our shared journey and comradery, and did I mention laughs? I was fortunate that as I grew older

Remember the value of an inspirational hand-written card.
– Kim Rich

Photo 29-2: My grandmothers Carolyn Allen, Grace Lindsey and Audrey Brock and me, May 1993

these women, who had also worked while raising a family, were able to retire and now support me in different ways, helping me with my new family and the changes that come with life. After the birth of my son, the caboose of our family, we made a decision to move from Louisiana (where I had lived my entire life) to Texas. The move, with a toddler and newborn baby, was tough, and without words or even an ask, Grandma Allen came along and helped my young family get established and provided the welcome structure and support that I need to start a new job in a new place.

Photo 29-3: Grandma Allen, me, Grandma Brock and my sister Kristi Cater, January 2010

I have one sister. She and I were both very close to our grandmas, and while there are no true favorites, as we reminisce about our grandmothers the stories that are most prevalent seem to focus on phrases, names or foods. Phrases like, "Odd Lots versus Big Lots," and names like why as the older grandchild I couldn't come up with something more exciting or matriarch-worthy, "grand-ma-ma" instead of just plain grandma, still make us laugh. As we shift to food, it's true my grandmothers could make a rubber boot taste good, another phrase frequently used. My place was solidified when Grandma Allen, planning a trip to Houston to visit her grands and great-grands, brought more than a suitcase. She packed a larder of my favorites: pot roast and tuna salad. My sister who lives just a mile away received a subsequent visit from Grandma. When asked what my sister wanted her to bring, of course my sister's answer was pot roast and tuna salad. Grandma arrived with a pork roast and chicken salad. Touché; I am beloved.

My last illustration of our special 'grand' bond filled a shoebox each year for four years of college. Every Wednesday when I picked up my mail, there waiting for me like clockwork was an inspirational card written in my grandma's hand with money inside, five dollars a week as a freshman, $10 as a sophomore, $15 during my junior year and twenty bucks as a senior. It became my fast food splurge or necessary gas cash or some other little something I could afford to buy because my grandma loved and remembered me every week. I knew I could depend on her, and those cards buoyed my spirits.

Photo 29-4: My sister Kristi, Grandma Lindsey and me, August 2010

My sister and I used to tease our grandmothers, and our Grandma Allen would say, "Y'all are gonna miss me when I'm gone." She couldn't have been more right. I have lost all my grandmother's over the past three years, and if I could reach back with a short letter to recognize their impact on me, it would simply say, "I hope you knew how much you impacted me; and I know how much love you had for me, but trust me, the love, respect and admiration I had for each of you was even greater."

Know how the company produces revenue and how each person impacts the bottom line. – Kim Rich

---

Strengths, solid work ethic, commitment, reward for a job well done and satisfaction for the accomplishment, all lessons taught by my grandmas, were reinforced by a key business mentor William (Bill) Ballard. When I first started work at CenterPoint Energy in the Accounting Department, Bill was the Chief Financial Officer. He made it clear with his assignments, behavior and words that he wanted more than bookkeepers. Rather, he expected analysts who could and would find areas for opportunity and improvement. He wanted his staff to initiate projects and drive them to completion. Bill saw the value in investing in his people, so we knew how the company produced revenue and how each person could impact the bottom line. We walked meter reading routes, we met crews installing utilities for new subdivisions, we trained to take payments and answer customer calls at service centers. Bill strived to develop an enterprise mindset among his accounting staff. He wanted us to see the big picture and how we fit in. I worked for Bill for seven years and realized that at some level, Bill could perform our jobs. He wasn't afraid to get his hands dirty or show that he was willing and able to learn other's duties. Bill could both walk the walk and talk the talk.

"Just because a decision is hard doesn't make the decision wrong. At times, a hard decision can sometimes be right."
— Kim Rich

Bill's lessons strongly influenced my career development. Being a woman and being in utility leadership, I understood, like Bill, that it's all about the work. Programs, initiatives and projects were happening around me, and I needed to proactively take responsibility for my path. That was the impetus that moved me from accounting to technology. There, I kept my nose down, learned and worked, following Bill's lesson plan. Colleagues asked me to join projects, to handle responsibilities, to step up to leadership roles. Working in this way, five plus years passed when I realized I was taking on leadership responsibilities but still in the same position. I had proven myself to be too valuable in my current role, and my own comfort and complacency had set in.

I was determined to prove my value beyond a keyboard role. I took steps to remind others that I had goals and wanted to achieve them. As I took control over my career, I was able to advance while continuing to provide value to key initiatives, just in a different capacity. The resilience I've had over the past few years is evident in the strength imbued from my grandmothers. I came to realize that it's okay to say no. I learned that just because a decision is hard doesn't make the decision wrong. At times, a hard decision can sometimes be right, and with my foundations of resiliency, dedication and hard work learned from Grandma Allen, Grandma Brock, Grandma Lindsey and reinforced by Bill, I've grown strong enough that even if I don't agree, I will get us where we need to go.

Kim Rich is a Customer Solutions Manager at CenterPoint Energy, a domestic energy delivery company headquartered in Houston, TX, that includes electric transmission and distribution, natural gas distribution and energy services operations. More than 7,400 CenterPoint Energy employees serve its gas and electric customers in Arkansas, Louisiana, Minnesota, Mississippi, Oklahoma and Texas, including the high-growth areas of Houston and Minneapolis. In April 2018, CenterPoint Energy, Inc. and Vectren Corporation announced a definitive merger agreement to form a leading energy delivery, infrastructure and services company serving more than 7 million customers across the United States.

CHAPTER 30

VINAY SHARMA
Chief Executive Officer
London Hydro

Photo 30-1: Vinay Sharma

Identifying and solving problems are hallmarks of great leaders. This valuable skillset, with its process models, logic paths and methodologies, can be learned at many fine schools, under tenured and respected teachers and from ancient and trendy curricula. My first exposure to problem-solving however was observed at my mother's knee. Anar Sharma, a single mother of five sons who taught high school math, showed how to address problems by her daily example. Practiced countless times for me and my brothers, her formula was simple: hard work, tenacity and task completion. I was a young boy in India observing her timeless values in actions, not hearing them in motherly lectures. I found myself unconsciously emulating and repeating them as I attended college in Canada: Do the

---

"Do the work, stay on task, complete assignments."
— Vinay Sharma

---

work, stay on task, complete assignments. Her values that I emulate today have borne me across oceans, brought academic achievement and positioned me again and again to lead large organizations to exceptional success.

As the youngest son, I naturally looked up to my brothers, especially my middle brother Lok because he carried my mother's example a step further. Her formula led to achievement; his ensured noble outcomes. In college at the time when I first realized his attitude, I saw Lok as the first to volunteer to sacrifice for the family. He would lead by stepping aside or pushing others forward. After I grew up and spent time with him in his home with his own family, I observed those sacrificial values again. His ability to surrender himself for others created a value system that informs my actions and decisions every day.

"Lead by stepping aside or pushing others forward."
– Vinay Sharma

Besides my mother and brother, two leaders taught me key lessons that significantly shaped that value system. Professor Ron Fleming of the University of Saskatchewan at Saskatoon was a total gentleman and a great influence upon me for the seven years I was there between 1980-87 and the nearly 30 years since. I completed my thesis under Ron Fleming's leadership. Not that he spoke to me or we officially interacted every day; rather, Ron Fleming taught me through his examples of kindness, honesty and a complete lack of pretension or need for recognition. Fleming was a well-accomplished professor in his own right, particularly around control systems, the "bread and butter" of engineers. While I continued to follow my mother's lessons as his student, what Ron Fleming taught me was the importance of connecting with others. Many situations with Fleming surprised me. One day in graduate school, I was working in Fleming's lab on an experiment when I unintentionally damaged some equipment. Scared to admit my silly mistake, I made my way to Professor Fleming's office and escorted him down to the lab for an explanation. I waited for his blame and criticism, but it was never delivered. Instead, Fleming engaged me in a conversation about the experiment. He asked me questions. We bantered back and forth about results. Professor Fleming and I were learning from each other. His demeanor was mentally exhilarating and removed all my fears. Of all my graduate school professors, Ron Fleming took the time that day in the middle of my embarrassing mistake to engage and learn together;

we were both students that day. My respect for him was immeasurable, and I think he respected me too.

Secondly, Leo Niekamp, an engineering manager, also influenced my early years as a design engineer at AMEC in Saskatoon. Niekamp's problem-solving method became a weekly tutorial on engagement. Most Fridays about 10 o'clock in the morning, he would call me into his office and throw out a problem. We would work on it together, identifying first principles, building logic and emerging with solutions that looped back and answered the problem. A senior manager, Niekamp already knew many of the answers, but he would take the time with me to teach the methodology. I internalized his process over the two years we worked together, and I use it today with the same results: teaching and engaging others to solve problems.

"Leadership is relationship. My natural tendencies are to show humility, to hold up a servant-like attitude, to relate to others openly and honestly, to break down not build up barriers." – Vinay Sharma

---

About eight years ago, my values honed from family and respected professionals were challenged by a bit of well-intentioned advice that I listened to but realized I could not emulate. When I became CEO of London Hydro in 2009, someone offered that I should maintain a professional distance from employees I was leading. By holding others at arm's length, I could maintain objectivity, manifest respect for myself and toward others, and not get bogged down in the details. I practiced the advice for a short time; it didn't and doesn't work for me. Leadership is relationship. My natural tendencies are to show humility, to hold up a servant-like attitude, to relate to others openly and honestly, to break down not build up barriers. I realized quickly that maintaining a professional distance was contradictory for me. The lessons I'd learned from my previous mentors overrode this advice.

I remain profoundly grateful for those mentioned here. If I could speak to each, I would say, "Just the way you lived your life left a legacy for me and others." In countless small ways, my mother Anar, my brother Lok, Professor Fleming and Leo Niekamp formed me into who I am. I thank them for their lessons of tenacity, selflessness, staying connected and engagement with others, values which I've embraced and routinely deploy to address the challenges utilities like London Hydro face today.

Serving 157,000-plus electricity customers and 113,000-plus water customers in London, Ontario, Canada, London Hydro is a wholly-owned subsidiary company that operates much like a private entity, so all Londoners essentially own the utility. In 2017, London Hydro received the Electricity Distributors Association's (EDA) Customer Service Excellence Award that recognizes the utility's Aeroplan Customer Loyalty Program and how it gives back to customers who take advantage of beneficial programs such as paperless billing and outage notifications. As Chief Executive Officer, Vinay Sharma proudly leads the capital and operational efforts necessary to enable innovative technologies that enhance customer experience.

10/8/2019

Kathy,
Thank you for being such an impactful leader and mentor to me throughout my career. I hope we continue to stay in touch!
Respectfully,
Bill

CHAPTER 31

BILL SHEPHERD
Chief Customer Officer
Gainesville Regional Utilities

Photo 31-1: Bill Shepherd

One of my earliest mentors was one of my high school football coaches. Coach Wright was a retired marine who looked and played the part very well. He was always clean shaven, hair cut high and tight, and clothes pressed and neat. His mere presence garnered respect from my first day on the practice field to my last game as a senior. Although I admired and respected most of my high school football coaches, Coach Wright held a special spot with a lot of us players. He was always "showing" us techniques and plays, not just telling us or writing it on the chalk board. When it came time to run

"High performance whether on the field or off requires hard work, diligence and practice. He also taught me through his actions that one of the best ways to gain respect and trust of your players (employees) is to roll up your sleeves, go shoulder to shoulder and be part of the unit."
– Bill Shepherd

Photo 31-2: Coach Wright, my high school football coach

wind sprints or stadiums at the end of practice, he was right there running with us. He was part of our unit which made him that much stronger of a leader.

Now I grew up in northern Illinois through junior high. "Yes, sir" and "No, sir" weren't part of my vocabulary. Not that I was disrespectful, but it just wasn't part of the culture in the north. From day one though, it was "Yes, Sir" and "No, Sir" to Coach Wright. His interaction with us and hands-on approach to coaching just made you want to please him and make him proud. He taught us lessons that I carry through life such as high performance whether on the field or off requires hard work, diligence and practice. He also taught me through his actions that one of the best ways to gain respect and trust of your players (employees) is to roll up your sleeves, go shoulder to shoulder and be part of the unit.

Photo 31-3: Kathy Viehe, my boss and then Interim General Manager at GRU

One of the most impactful mentors during my utility career was Kathy Viehe. I was fortunate enough that until her retirement, she was also my boss during most of my time here at Gainesville Regional Utilities. She taught me valuable lessons in humility, employee engagement and navigating the local political climate.

The lesson in humility was a tough one and came early in my managerial career. A director position had come open which I felt was a natural fit for me and a logical progression from where I was. I prepared by talking to the previous director as well as some employees of the departments which that director oversaw.

However, when it came time to interview, I didn't do a good job at all selling my skills and abilities. Since I knew all the folks on the panel, of which my boss was one of them, I assumed they were all keenly aware of my "superior abilities and exceptional acumen." As such, I left all my value proposition out of the conversation. Needless to say, someone else interviewed that left nothing off the table and got the job.

After getting the devastating news, I went to my boss and asked what happened. She said, "I waited the whole time for you to start selling yourself and showcase your abilities and you didn't. When you get to this level, you cannot make any assumptions that others know your abilities, you must always be ready to sell your abilities especially in an interview."

Now I could have sulked around and blamed everyone else for not noticing my "obvious" value to the company, but I didn't. I continued to hone my skills and become an even better manager and when that job opened up three years later, guess what? I left nothing off the table and got the job. I never hesitate to share that lesson with my employees. Just because you think you possess the skills necessary doesn't mean everyone else knows it. Leave nothing off the table!

"You cannot make any assumptions that others know your abilities, you must always be ready to sell your abilities."
– Bill Shepherd

I'll try really hard to protect the not-so-innocent, so I won't get into too much detail, but this lesson definitely falls into the "Please Don't Emulate" category. I'll call this the "Sharpen Iron with Iron" lesson. A new executive to our company had recently started and quickly got involved with a key project. This project was struggling and came to a critical moment in time where we had to pick between two alternatives. The vendor was there in full force presenting the alternatives. Midway through the vendor's presentation, key internal members of the project took their turn explaining the benefits and drawbacks of both options. At some point during the presentation, this executive and two others had a sidebar conversation and had made up their minds that option A was where we were going. Unfortunately, just before this private epiphany, one of the junior managers in the room who reported to me was in the middle of explaining why option B was the best way to go. The new executive became very agitated and in a condescending way proceeded to question me as to why I'm letting my manager continue to speak, to which my response was, "He has just as much right to speak as anyone else." Shortly after, that executive shut down the meeting and asked if we could talk afterwards.

Now, I'm very protective of my folks and don't take kindly to employees, whether or not at fault, being ridiculed by a superior in a group setting. I shared my view with this executive and his response was: I see a lot of potential in him (the manager) and sometimes the best way to develop them is to sharpen iron with iron. In other words, treating them badly when they have opposing opinions will somehow cultivate professional development. Please don't emulate that behavior. In addition to being open-minded and welcoming to other's opinions, I subscribe to the good ol' fashioned saying, "Praise publicly and criticize privately."

"A great leader surrounds themselves with folks that are smarter than they are. It's the leader's job to break down barriers and cultivate them so they can work their magic."
– Bill Shepherd

Needless to say, the executive and I just had to agree to disagree, but I then had to approach my manager and reassure him that his viewpoint was valuable and to not let that experience change that. Although he took it like a champ, some time needed to lapse before he felt comfortable sharing his opinions again with that particular executive.

We as leaders cannot afford to snub ideas or viewpoints from the very people who support us. A great leader surrounds themselves with folks that are smarter than they are. It's the leader's job to break down barriers and cultivate them so they can work their magic.

To Kathy, I would write a letter saying the same thing I said to her when she retired:

Kathy,

I have been fortunate to have you as my boss during most of my professional career. I thank you for being a tremendous mentor, boss and friend. The humility I have, the way I treat my employees and the way I navigate tricky situations is due in large part to the values you've demonstrated and instilled in me. I can only hope that I'm as successful at passing on those values to others as you were to me. Thank you!

Bill Shepherd is the Chief Customer Officer of Gainesville Regional Utilities, Florida's fifth largest municipal utility providing electric, natural gas, water, wastewater and telecommunications services to approximately 93,000 retail and wholesale customers in Gainesville and surrounding areas. Its mission is based on four core business values: safety, efficiency, environmental responsibility and professionalism. Gainesville Regional Utilities prides itself on being environmentally responsible, community-minded, safe and reliable.

CHAPTER 32

TONY SIMAS
Director – Call Center (Retired)
Eversource

Photo 32-1: Tony Simas

I was born and raised in the Azores in the mid-1950s, until I moved to the U.S. with my family when I was age 15. In the Azores, my father Jose Simas grew pineapples and bananas. He had an average of 10 men working for him in the fields or green houses. From dad, I learned the following lessons:

Lead by Example: In the fields or green houses, my dad would go over the work for the day with the crew. Often as I brought lunch, I would see him working side by side with the crew. He would eat his lunch at the same time and take the same allotted time to eat the meal as his men. Also, he only took breaks when the team did.

Respect Everyone: In Azores as I was growing up, it was customary and expected when you came across a priest, teacher or person of social/economic status to acknowledge that person, and if you were a male, to remove your hat. My family was considered to be upper middle class; however, that did not stop by dad from removing his hat when he greeted an older

Photo 32-2: My father, Jose Simas

Photo 32-3: My daughter, Danielle

person regardless of their economic status. My dad instilled in us, regardless of the person's background, that you treat them with respect.

Include Others: In our household we had help to clean the house, wash clothes and perform other domestic duties. During meal time, social custom dictated that the help was expected to eat in the kitchen alone. In our home, the help ate with us and contributed to the conversation.

Live Life to the Fullest: My daughter Danielle loved life and travel. Even when our children were very young, as a family twice a year we would travel to the Caribbean, Europe or the U.S. Shortly after returning from vacation, she would ask us when and where we planned to go next. Danielle was blind to people's ethnicity; many of her friends were from different countries which inspired her to learn about their cultures. Unfortunately, in 2000, we lost Danielle at age 17 to a car accident. In her short life, she taught me to live life to the fullest and accept people for what they are, because from one moment to the next, life can change or end.

"During meal time, social custom dictated that the help was expected to eat in the kitchen alone. In our home, the help ate with us and contributed to the conversation."
– Tony Simas

Dear Danielle,

This is the first time I've written you since you tragically passed away after a car accident 18 years ago. There are so many emotions I want to put in my letter, but at this time I want to focus on a few lessons you taught me, especially the one that says, "Live life to the fullest, because life is too short." There were several events in your life I missed, and I'm sorry; but after your death, I made sure I did not miss any of your brother's. What a horrible price I had to pay! You had such a positive outlook on challenges. You saw the possibilities not the abilities. Danielle, for the last 18 years, I have not taken things for granted and instead appreciate things no matter how small or insignificant they may seem. I do not know if you know this, but you inspired me to retire earlier, because life is too short. Finally, Danielle, it is important for people to know that I'm writing this letter not because you died; I write because you lived!

Forever in my heart,
Dad

"Live life to the fullest and accept people for what they are, because from one moment to the next, life can change or end." – Tony Simas

---

Photo 32-4: Archie Christopher (Chris), my early mentor

Photo 32-5: My mentor Jonathan Carey, manager of customer care at Commonwealth Gas

Embrace Diversity: In the early 1970s, throughout high school and college, I worked part-time at night for a Boston-based cleaning company for seven years. All the employees were 100% on part-time status. For the majority of them, this was their second job, and most were first generation from Western Europe. After three years working there, the director Archie Christopher (whom we called Chris), promoted me to supervisor, and one of my responsibilities was hiring. Chris, an African American, mentored me on the hiring process and eventually allowed me to hire people on my own. He stressed to me the importance of hiring people of different ethnicities and giving them an opportunity to supplement their income. As I looked at the approximately 40 employees, 85% were from Western Europe. Chris's comment made me aware of the situation through his eyes, so I made a point of hiring people of various backgrounds and cultures.

In in the mid-1980s, Jonathan Carey, a manager of customer care at Commonwealth Gas, part of Commonwealth Energy System, gave me the opportunity to join the management team. He was my mentor for years to come. He helped me develop and strengthen the following skills:

> "A good leader is available and should never be too busy to listen to someone regardless of their role." – Tony Simas

Show Sincere Concern: Through his daily interactions with peers or employees, Jonathan encouraged me as a good leader to genuinely care about people and help them do their best.

Promote Collaboration: During meetings, union negotiations or conversation in general, he taught me the importance of giving everyone an opportunity to participate and comment on their ideas. He lived out the value that working along with someone or a group to achieve a common goal promoted opportunities for recognition and respect for each other.

Show Consideration: Jonathan reinforced to me that one needs to understand that, at times, events in life goes wrong, and we to need give people time to deal with life's problems.

Be Accessible: Jonathan understood that a good leader is available and should never be too busy to listen to someone regardless of their role. Jonathan pointed out to me that if I'm visible, it demonstrates to people that I'm also accessible to the team. This quality to me is paramount especially during a reorganization, procedure and policy change.

Currently, a CS Week LeadNext coach, Tony Simas retired in 2016 as the Director of the Call Center at Eversource, a Fortune 500 regional energy and water company in the New England states of Connecticut, Massachusetts and New Hampshire. Its 8,000 employees deliver electricity, natural gas and water services to approximately 4 million customers. Eversource cultivates a wide social media presence on Facebook, Flickr, Instagram, Twitter and YouTube, in addition to traditional call center contact and consumer communications, so its large customer base receives timely service and useful information.

CHAPTER 33

KAREN SPARKMAN
Director, Customer Experience Operations
TECO

Photo 33-1: Karen Sparkman

My mother Annamaria was my mentor from a young age. She taught me to always be kind to others, take the time to understand differing perspectives and look at life through diverse lenses, without applying judgment. She also taught me that life isn't always fair and that there would be times where the outcome was beyond our level of control and, when that occurred, we must make the best of whatever situation we find ourselves in. I truly believe these lessons have stuck with me through my adult life and have helped me to be a better parent, spouse, sibling, leader, etc. Whenever I am faced with tough situations, I always think back to the lessons that have shaped me and made me the person I am today, and I apply those learned principles.

During the early years of my career, I was fortunate enough to have a mentor that was strong, ambitious, influential and believed in me and

> "Look at life through diverse lenses, without applying judgment." – Karen Sparkman

Photo 33-2: My mother Annamaria and me

my potential to be an effective servant leader. She taught me several key lessons that included: valuing people, looking at failure as an opportunity to grow/learn/do better next go-around and always putting others' success in front of my own. She also taught me to take my strengths and use them to help others fill their gaps. She was hard on me at times, assigning stretch goals and assignments that seemed insurmountable to achieve, but she always stood beside me, offering guidance on next steps, helping me to learn, developing my skillsets and growing in my craft.

> "She also taught me to take my strengths and use them to help others fill their gaps." – Karen Sparkman

When I worked in the telecommunications industry as a young, green leader, I had a mentor tell me that leadership was strictly about managing the roles and responsibilities of those that report to you. As I grew into my role, I slowly learned this couldn't be further from the truth. I learned instead that being an effective leader has more to do with inspiring others and helping them to grow and flourish in their own right. This same person would also tell me to make sure I hired team members who had the same strengths as me. Again, I learned the complete opposite was true and have since focused on building teams with diverse backgrounds, as well as strengths and weaknesses that I could learn and grow from. While she meant well in her intentions, the lessons were not right for the leader I aspired to be.

If I could write a letter to my mentors, I would thank each of them for being in my life during the times I needed them the most. I would tell them they are the reason I am who I am today because they did not give up on me. They walked beside me until I was able to stand on my own and be a leader and mentor within my own right. Whenever I felt as if I could not do something, they encouraged me and pushed me in the right direction.

> Focus on building teams with diverse backgrounds, as well as strengths and weaknesses to learn and grow from."
> – Karen Sparkman

They are the reason I am successful today. Lastly, I would thank them for always believing in me, even through those times when I was struggling to believe in myself.

Karen Sparkman is the Director of Customer Experience Operations for TECO Energy, a leading energy company located in Tampa, FL, and a subsidiary of Emera Inc., a geographically diverse energy and services company headquartered in Halifax, Nova Scotia, Canada. Three core businesses build TECO's service delivery portfolio: Tampa Electric, a regulated utility serving more than 756,000 customers; Peoples Gas System, the state's largest natural gas distributor with more than 386,000 customers; and New Mexico Gas Co., a natural gas distributor and the largest utility in New Mexico serving more than 515,000 customers.

CHAPTER 34

JERRY SULLIVAN
CIO and Vice President
Orlando Utilities Commission

Photo 34-1: Jerry Sullivan

I have always craved to learn more – whether from a book, an experience, a person or a relationship. My earliest childhood experiences in the mountains and hills of western and northern New York and my interactions with my family sparked what became a lifetime obsession of learning.

I grew up during the time when we were out of the house at sunrise and parents only had to say be home when the street lights go on. On my brother's hand-me-down English Racer (the coolest bicycle around), I raced over every hill, through every wood and down every path for miles around. What I couldn't experience before the street lights went on, I discovered through reading.

When you are young, things are simple. I had a small paper route with 27 customers, small enough to allow me time to explore the hills and play games with my friends. I made enough money to get an Italian Ice every day. What more did a boy need? Delivering papers eventually made me curious about what was inside these papers and what was outside of New York?

I started to read the front page of the newspaper and became very knowledgeable about current events before eventually moving on to the opinion pieces and editorials. When the newspaper wasn't enough, I moved on to an encyclopedia. I read the entire 17-volume *Golden Book Encyclopedia* from cover to cover, several times. Through the journalists' and writers' eyes, I felt like I knew John Kennedy, Lyndon Johnson, Barry Goldwater, Richard Nixon, Spiro Agnew and Nelson Rockefeller even though I never met them. People can inspire us to do great things; other's lives inspire us to make good decisions. Even affluent doctors in town you have never met – doctors who drove a Chrysler Imperial or the rare Cadillac Eldorado and lived in houses a bit better than the rest of ours – can inspire you. I remember the cars and the houses well. Would I ever own one?

"Find your best traits and use them." – Jerry Sullivan

I left New York state long ago, but I am still thankful for the influences there that instilled in me a desire to achieve, learn everything I could and strive for the best, starting with my family. My parents were always encouraging, and the natural competition with my siblings for our parents' appreciation and affection was motivating. When I was four, I remember listening to my parents work with my older brother on math skills such as multiplication tables and addition/subtraction problems. As an adult, I realize now that memorizing the answers and yelling them out before my brother was a terrific game for me but not so much for my brother. I suspect my often-unchecked pesky sibling behavior may have led to the instigator personality and memorization skills that characterize me today. It certainly made me aware that both traits are often at odds with my relationship with my older brother. We get older and wiser, and I am glad there was a lesson in this: relationships and feelings of others are the most important attributes in personal and professional successes.

The combination of worldly events embedded in the *Encyclopedia* and my earnest desire to memorize my older brother's school lessons shaped my interests in science, technology, engineering and math. Sound trite? STEM? Really, Jerry? This is probably not the classic way of an early exposure to STEM, but it certainly shaped my desire to learn and be competitive at the same time.

My earliest memories of teachers that made a difference in my life, how I looked at the world and what I could accomplish were at my junior high school. I vividly remember Mrs. Simcovitz who taught history and a sense of wanderlust. Mrs. Simcovitz travelled the world and said the best place on earth was New Zealand. Wow, I had to learn about that country! Prior to teaching, she was an interpreter at the famed and historic post-World War II Nuremburg trials. I listened to every word she ever said, about anything. In English class, Mr. Raymond developed my writing skills with numerous book reports and essays. He instilled in me a love of prose and literature that pulled me away from newspaper stories.

"'Do your homework.'" – Jerry Sullivan

I went from small public schools located in old country towns to a large public high school with thousands of students. It would have been easy to become complacent. Competition was scant, recognition was scanter and the middle-class housing developments made everyone feel safe, if not the same. Exceling in school when surrounded by a majority who just wanted to finish was effortless. The yearning to learn more, however, to become more, was always the vexing proposition. How do you get the big break, the opportunity to accomplish great things and to attend the best schools? Life far away from New York City is peaceful and calm but a difficult locale to carve out a living. My father relocated the family to Phoenix, Arizona, and my life dramatically changed.

I had my lucky high school break when my parents enrolled me in a Jesuit high school, Brophy College Preparatory. A top school in Phoenix, Brophy accepted boys from different backgrounds and economic levels; academics were the main requirement for acceptance. My new friends I met there – some rich, some poor – became mentors as well. We all took and competed in Latin, Calculus, Psychology and World Religions.

Photo 34- 2: Father Anton J. Renna, S.J., my teacher and mentor

Father Anton J. "Sam" Renna, S.J. was a beloved teacher, mentor and spiritual guide I met while at Brophy. He was one of the most inspiring, most influential and most intriguing people I ever met. He assigned us works of Chaucer, Shakespeare and Dante. We read *The Canterbury Tales* which I recall as being a narrative about "sondry folk" making their leisurely way to Canterbury. I couldn't fathom that pilgrims had such dubious characters on the way to Canterbury and on their return.

Father Renna and my other instructors prepared me for my next adventure. While there, I applied to the US Military Academy at West Point. A full four-year scholarship, plus a job as a 2nd Lieutenant, were mine if only I could

Photo 34- 3: U.S. Military Academy - West Point, Class of 1976 Cadet Company: F2

get accepted. With encouragement from my parents, I applied through people I only knew from my "newspaper days," Senators Barry Goldwater or Paul Fannin. I was accepted, and my next adventure began.

West Point leadership training is known throughout the military, and there is a process that every cadet goes through. My West Point associates/classmates were great role models. Our class had more generals than any other in the Academy's 215-year history. One classmate, General Odierno was appointed the Chief of Staff of the Army. My squad leader, Martin Dempsey became the Chairman of the Joint Chiefs. My long-time West Point roommate Bruce Jette was recently sworn in as the Assistant Secretary of the Army for Acquisition, Logistics and Technology. I was in very good company, and I hope that I learned a thing or two including the fact that mentors can come from all around you – your bosses, your colleagues and your direct reports.

Photo 34-4: General of the Army Omar Bradley, my mentor who spoke about 10 leadership principles

My tactical officer, Major Courtney Rittgers (Class of '61) and aide to America's last five-star General, Omar Bradley, taught me that relationships, leadership and integrity were more important attributes than learning physics, law, chemistry and engineering. I had plenty of classes in the latter and four long years of 24 x 7 training in the former.

After I graduated, Major Rittgers continued to be an inspiration and a mentor. Years later, he promoted me to the rank of Captain in Omar Bradley's office. I seized the opportunity to ask General Bradley to speak to our Captain's class on leadership. General Bradley accepted and spoke about ten leadership principles. He provided lofty and interesting descriptions of Churchill, Eisenhower, Patton, Montgomery, Roosevelt and others, and he described those he knew personally and who best characterized each leadership principle. The major lesson was that few people have all ten traits; most just have one. After the lecture, I remember his advice to me: find your best traits and use them.

I eventually became a paratrooper platoon leader and a commander in the elite 82nd Airborne Division. My battalion commander and Korean War veteran, Lieutenant Colonel James McKnight, was an inspiring leader who set high standards while providing encouragement and recognition. Under his command, we were recognized as the best unit in the Corps. After a one-year stint in Korea, I returned as the Commander of my paratrooper unit and completed 137 jumps (over 100 with combat equipment) to become a Master Parachutist. It's a badge with great honor in the military but with little recognition in civilian life. I was nevertheless a happy person.

I next transitioned from active duty into the Army Reserves as the Aide to Major General William Sylvester. I was very young, and he was a World War II veteran. He seemed to know everyone's name and every detail of every organization in his 100-unit, 10,000-person command. If there was ever a leader that I watched closely, it was this general who made everyone feel important, and he listened to every issue and took action on things that mattered.

Photo 34-5: Brigadier General John Jannarone, my mentor who saw a succession planning gap at Consolidated Edison

Outside the Army, my next role set the course for the remainder of my career when I joined New York City-based utility Consolidated Edison (Con Ed) as a young engineer. The former academic dean while I was at West Point, Brigadier General John Jannarone, had joined Con Ed, as a vice president. He saw a succession planning gap at Con Edison's senior ranks and decided to hire young captains in the military to start seeding the management ranks at the lower levels. Earlier in his Army career, Jannarone was the special assistant to the Commanding General of the famed Manhattan Project, the most notable engineering achievement in the 20th century. Captains (including myself) were eager to join him at Con Edison. I became the Superintendent for the Bronx Division and later becoming the engineer and Superintendent for Westchester and finally Manager, Central Operations (Fossil and Nuclear).

General Public Utilities (GPU, now First Energy) was my next career stop where I honed my management skills under the tutelage of Senior Vice

President Allen Donofrio. His attention to detail and experience were invaluable in shaping my utility acumen. His knowledge of utilities was among the best I've come across.

To further myself, I next pursued and earned an MBA in Finance from New York University's Leonard N. Stern School of Business. While there, I met W. Edwards Deming, an American engineering, statistician, management consultant and NYU's most notable professor. When I asked him a question on probability and statistics, his simple response was a lesson I never forgot: "Do your homework, Mr. Sullivan."

Photo 34-6: Dr. Joyce Orsini, Deming's graduate assistant and one of my mentors

While still at GPU, we hired Joyce Orsini (Deming's graduate assistant and now a professor at Fordham) to assist GPU Nuclear turn around two nuclear power plants, TMI-1 and Oyster Creek. Her leadership, wisdom and methodologies helped these generating stations reach some of the highest capacity factors in the world. She helped institute a culture of measurement, outcomes, analysis and a fact-based management style. I had the fortunate opportunity to speak to her recently, and she reminisced how people and culture were part of Deming's philosophy for improving corporate outcomes. This was so true; I (and our GPU Nuclear Company) was fortunate to be a student of such notable mentors and professors. He was professor at NYU while I was there, and his persona was Deming's mentorship to her, and her mentorship to many of my company employees is an education people can only wish for.

I next joined an international consulting firm where I continued learning about utilities in the U.S. and abroad. I was exposed to clients of the US Aid for International Development (USAID) and World Bank clients. It was fascinating to hear about major client countries putting forth their ideas for development. My most interesting assignment was working for the Republic of South Africa, during the post-Nelson Mandela period. The new president, President Mbeki wanted several things in the electric industry: 1) create a holding company to oversee the industry, 2) restructure the 187 electric municipalities into six regions, 3) provide new generation and 4) provide electricity for the townships. I became the advisor for the CEO of that nation's electric distribution industry.

As a part of my work in South Africa, I wrote a paper, *The Four Tenets for Electric Industry Restructuring.* It detailed how to accomplish restructuring by improving customer payments, lowering long term debt, raising

Value a culture of measurement, outcomes, analysis and fact-based management. – Jerry Sullivan

capital and lowering expenses and providing electricity to the impoverished. It was met with wide acclaim and recognition. I was at a symposium in Pretoria, and I couldn't believe my instant notoriety and fame about writing such a "wonderful" and enlightening case for restructuring. I suspect, however, much of my fame was mistaken for another namesake, Leon Sullivan. It was this Mr. Sullivan who gained recognition for writing the *Sullivan Principles*, the bible on how South Africa could succeed in post-apartheid. Nevertheless, President Mbeki was on the right track, and I was happy to support the initiative, and a bit of innocent but mistaken identity still helps.

Exposure to different people, different school systems and an encouraging family has characterized my experience. Learning, enticed by the immense satisfaction of interacting with great minds, always gave me the greatest sense of accomplishment. The sense of satisfaction and thrill from a lifelong learning crusade is a high that shapes the way I live, work and play. The adrenaline high from playing a modern video game is short-lived by comparison, a lesson I hope the next generation finds.

AKA, OUC-The Reliable One, Orlando Utilities Commission is located in one of the most visited places in the world. OUC is the second largest municipal utility in Florida. Serving a customer base of 435,000 and a population of over 1.9 million, this utility of about 1,100 employees has invested heavily in forward-thinking technology improvements for its customers in Orlando, St. Cloud and parts of Orange and Osceola counties. It is a leader of firsts: number one status in reliability since 1998 based on data from the Florida Public Service Commission; first to convert to ozone water treatment; first solar farm in Orange County and the State's first solar panels on utility poles; first solar-powered electric vehicle charging stations; and Central Florida's first community solar farm. Jerry Sullivan as CIO and Vice President has implemented, enabled and now maintains these operational technologies.

CHAPTER 35

DAVE TOMLINSON
CS Week LeadNext Coach
CS Week

Photo 35-1: Dave Tomlinson

T he first leader who taught me about business was my boss at my part-time job in high school. I worked at a Firestone store, and the owner's name was Jack Fenter. He taught me so many things that ultimately led to my pursuing a career in business. Jack trusted me thoroughly, often using me to fill in as manager when he was away on vacation, supervising mechanics much older than me, resolving customer inquiries, sales and complaints. He taught me how to balance the books of the business and deal with vendors. Jack instilled the importance of treating the customer fairly and providing honest value. Jack was a marketing expert and taught me the value of advertising and how to promote the business in a competitive environment. However, Jack also encouraged me to continue my education instead of choosing a career with him. He saw the value in learning both academically and by getting personally involved with the work. Looking back on the experience, I'm so grateful that he took a teenager under his wing, trusted me and gave me the opportunity to learn.

One of the best mentors I ever experienced was my boss at the time, Lynette Vermillion. She taught me many lessons, but the ones I remember most were:

1. Always have time for your employees;

2. When you are thinking... "Someone should do something about...", that someone is YOU!; and

3. "Don't focus on where you spent your time, tell me what you changed or accomplished."

Lynette always made time for her team, even during her busiest moments. She was a strong people person who formed personal relationships with her staff and always used humor to lighten the mood when things were going tough. She formed relationships with her staff and was willing to provide support and leadership through difficult situations. This lesson was critical to my success when later in my career I served as a Call Services Manager. I suddenly had 150 employees who needed my time, and I had a long list of administrative responsibilities. Remembering Lynette's lessons on dealing with people was a lesson that served me well during that time.

"'When you are thinking... Someone should do something about..., that someone is YOU!'" – Dave Tomlinson

---

When I worked with Lynette, we were in a staff role at the time, and it was easy to find things that different parts of the organization should do differently or how a process should be changed in Customer Service. Lynette empowered us to make a difference in the company and encouraged us to challenge the process. When we talked about something that needed changing, Lynette made it very clear that her expectation was that we actively pursued making that change. This led to Lynette's saying, "When you say... Someone should do something about..., that someone is YOU!"

The utility industry at the time focused a lot on civic involvement, attending meetings and generally being involved in the community. Many times, employees were promoted for attending a lot of meetings or simply getting face time. Lynette's philosophy was a culture change for our company. She emphasized, "Don't simply tell me about the things you observed or meetings you attended. Tell me what you changed, what did you make better, what actions did you take, what did you accomplish?" This was radical for the time but prepared me for what would come later in my career as we experienced mergers, acquisitions and major change within the industry.

> ### "'Don't focus on where you spent your time; instead, communicate what you changed or accomplished.'"
> ### – Dave Tomlinson

Lynette also empowered me to do my job and didn't micromanage me every step of the way. What a great experience it is to have someone who trusts you to do a job and empowers you to make it happen! Nothing is worse than someone giving you an assignment and then trying to do it for you.

Lynette's guidance and coaching were keys to my accomplishing a 35 plus-year career and being successful with a wide range of expectations.

I believe each mentor provides both positive examples of behaviors to follow as well as behaviors that are not always the most beneficial. We have the ability to pick and choose the behaviors we want to emulate and those we want to avoid.

I've had two mentors who felt a PowerPoint presentation was never good enough. They believed the presentations should be rehearsed, tweaked, changed and modified all the way to the point of delivery. I vividly recall working until 10 or 11 pm on a presentation, then changing it back to a version from earlier in the day. I have grown to appreciate the phrase, "Don't let the desire to be perfect get in the way of delivering a great product." In retrospect, I know these leaders were using the presentation development as a way to focus on delivering a very high-quality product and maybe even to spend time bonding over a work project. However, this often resulted in my frustration and a feeling of wasted time. I don't ever want a direct report or business associate to feel that I'm wasting their time.

> ### "'Don't let the desire to be perfect get in the way of delivering a great product.'" – Dave Tomlinson

Another mentor I had was so focused on personal development, he could waste all day discussing career opportunities, classes we could take or ways to learn more about the business. While personal development is a wonderful aspect of a mentor, it can be overdone and any skill that is overdone becomes a liability. He was a self-proclaimed mentor to everyone in the company. While he was someone who offered a lot in the ways of self-development, he also started to develop a reputation as someone to avoid.

Knowing when a skill has been overdone is critical to long term success and relationship building.

If I could share a letter with my mentors, I'd say,

Dear Jack/Lynette,

During the time we worked together, I learned so many lessons that served me well later in my career. I also want you to know how much of a difference you made in my personal life and career and that many of the things you taught me have been passed down to others as I assumed a greater leadership role in the company. You and many of the employees I mentored will likely never meet or know each other, but you should know that many of the lessons you taught me will live on through mergers, acquisitions and a new generation. I've already seen evidence of these lessons being passed along by the folks I mentored.

Each of you has many attributes in common:

1. You are laser focused on people and being effective communicators,

2. You are focused on achieving results,

3. You care about others and are willing to help,

4. You trust others to do their jobs and avoid the temptation of micromanaging them day to day, and

5. I wanted to do a good job for you because of our relationship.

Each of you prepared me early in my career for effectively dealing with the many challenges I faced later, even though I didn't realize it at the time. You have no idea of how many times I have thought about the lessons you taught me as I was dealing with an employee or other issue.

I appreciate your best efforts to make me successful. I am writing this letter to make sure you know how I much I valued our relationship, your mentoring and your concern. The lessons you taught me have been passed down and will live in the next generation.

None of us ever knows the total impact we've made on other's lives. I hope you know how much of a difference you made in mine.

Dave

Dave Tomlinson is a CS Week LeadNext coach, responsible for coaching a select group of high-potential employees from various utilities through a 12-month curriculum that includes CS Week Conference attendance, webinars and site visits. The LeadNext program utilizes a coaching relationship where participants acquire deeper knowledge and broader understanding of all aspects of utility customer service. Before his retirement from Duke Energy in 2016, Dave served in a wide range of customer service leadership roles throughout his lengthy career.

CHAPTER 36

JOE TRENTACOSTA
SVP & CIO
Southern Maryland Electric Cooperative

Photo 36-1: Joe Trentacosta

An early mentor of mine was my grandfather. He owned a poultry market in the Bronx. When I was 10 years old, he would bring me down to the market during school breaks to earn a little money and, more importantly, learn a little about business. He thought it was very important that I learn how to handle money and deal with customers, even at this early age. So, one of the first lessons he taught me was how to take cash payments and make change. Occasionally, I would also take orders over the phone. My time working at his poultry market had the double benefit for me of learning how to deal with customers and learning about finance. This valuable experience was no doubt a key reason why I wanted to pursue a career in 'business' as I got older.

Hard work and dedication were two values I learned by watching my parents. My father was a police officer for the NYPD and watching his weekly grind of around the clock shift work instilled in me the value that nothing beats a hard day's work. I saw him take on odd jobs (like selling fire

Photo 36-2: Me with a yo-yo, sister Rosemarie and Grandpa at Grandpa Ro Joe Chicken Market

Photo 36-3: Mom and Dad (in his NYPD uniform)

alarms and smoke detectors) just to make ends meet. All the while my mother was fully committed to raising the kids, and her dedication to that task never wavered. But, most importantly, if they experienced any issues, financial or otherwise, they never burdened the kids with it. Through their eyes, the sky was truly the limit for their children, and the future held endless possibilities. If you can dream it, you can do it. This was a valuable lesson, one I have tried to pass along to my daughter. I came across this quote a few years ago and hung it on the refrigerator in our home so my teenage daughter could see it every day. It was what my parents were trying to teach me through their actions, but without saying it quite so eloquently. *"Don't limit yourself. Many people limit themselves to what they think they can do. You go as far as your mind lets you. What you believe, remember, you can achieve."* – Mary Kay Ash

I have always viewed my business career as being shaped by the many mentors I have worked for, directly or indirectly, over the years. When I have received good advice, I have often found myself giving that same advice to someone else, sometimes many years later.

Some of the key lessons I learned early were from the president of the first company I worked for full-time after graduating college. His name was Jack Brennan, and he was the President of Metro Mobile, an up-and-coming cellular telephone organization headquartered in NYC in the mid-1980s.

In the summer of 1984, I interviewed with Mr. Brennan for a part-time position as their first information systems employee. During the interview, he asked me if I had any questions. Being young and naïve, I asked him if he could tell me exactly what kind of company Metro Mobile was.

"It's up to you to chart your own path." – Joe Trentacosta

Career Lesson #1: Never ask this question during an interview! His response told me my question was inappropriate, "I don't know," he jokingly replied, "but if you ever figure it out, you let me know." While I did get the job, this quickly led to

Career Lesson #2: Nobody's going to hand you anything. All careers are not going to start with some formalized training program. Sometimes, you are going to be thrown into a position, maybe at a startup company or in some new department, with minimal guidance, and only a user manual for some off-the-shelf software. It's up to you to chart your own path. If you are going to succeed, you need initiative. This is a key trait, and something I still look for today when interviewing perspective employees.

As the cellular industry was exploding, Metro Mobile was rapidly expanding in the Northeast, Southeast and Southwest regions of the U.S. At the time, I was in my early 20s and I was working for a subsidiary company of Metro Mobile that was in the process of being sold, so my job in NYC at corporate headquarters was going away. As a result, I was offered an IT job at the Northeast region headquarters (located in Connecticut) of this rapidly growing cellular company (which now, many years later and through many acquisitions and mergers, is Verizon Wireless). This would require me to leave my comfort zone of New York, where I was born and raised. I expressed my hesitation to relocate to Mr. Brennan, who told me that I shouldn't be so risk averse, especially at such a young age. There would be plenty of time for that, he shared, as I moved on in my life and in my career. He advised that career opportunities should be evaluated for what they are, not where they are. So, I took the job and started the daily commute to the Connecticut office.

"If you can dream it, you can do it." – Joe Trentacosta

As it turns out, this was sound advice from Mr. Brennan. It was counsel that has served me well throughout my career, including when I accepted an IT Director position (career advancement at the time) at the Verizon Wireless Washington/Baltimore region headquarters in Silver Spring, Maryland, without even making a site visit. At the time, I was living in New Jersey, and this new job had the potential of being a good career move. So, I just picked up and relocated. As it turned out, that director position was a key turning point in my quest to someday become a CIO.

Regarding that potential move to Connecticut so many years ago, well, that lasted all of two days. On the third day I received a call offering me an IT Manager position back at the Metro Mobile NYC headquarters office due to an unexpected vacancy. However, while my tenure in Connecticut was short, the lesson has lasted a lifetime.

It's hard to imagine that even in the mid-1980s this next story would have been considered acceptable behavior. Very early in my career as a young IT manager, I had a boss who was frustrated over a system issue that we were having. I was working with a contractor on the issue when my boss (my "mentor" at the time) approached us to discuss the problem. During the course of the discussion, he attempted to provide some direction, which was very unclear. When I sought clarification, he grabbed my head and mocked blowing in my ear in an attempt to see if it was empty, i.e., 'Do you have any brains in there?' Needless to say, in addition to being a classic "do not emulate" behavior, this did not improve my credibility with the contractor. Fortunately, as embarrassing as it was, I always looked back on this as a valuable lesson to guide me as my career progressed.

> "Career opportunities should be evaluated for what they are, not where they are." – Joe Trentacosta

---

Career Lesson #3: Always treat everyone with dignity and respect. Looking back, I'm so grateful to have learned such a valuable lesson at such a young and impressionable point in my career.

My mentors have taught me lasting lessons. If I could address a few words to each one mentioned here, I'd say:

To my grandfather: Thanks for having the vision to teach me business lessons at such a young and impressionable age. They have served me well.

To my parents: Thanks for setting such a positive example and teaching me lessons that last a lifetime, regardless of where life and my career take me.

To Jack Brennan: Who knew I would still be reflecting thirty years later on a moment in my first career interview? I will never forget the opportunity you afforded me as a young college student, including the full-time job offer (my first) you made to me at the intersection of 59th Street and Park Avenue as we walked back from lunch. It was a start of what continues to be an exciting and rewarding career.

To the boss that embarrassed me in front of a contractor: Sometimes gifts come in the strangest of packages, and if you are lucky, the truly great ones keep on giving. The gift of the unfortunate way you choose to coach me has made me a better manager, and others I have supervised over the years have benefited from it.

Joe Trentacosta is both Chief Information Officer and Senior Vice President of Customer and Enterprise Services, an unusual but effective role pairing, for Southern Maryland Electric Cooperative (SMECO). As his own customer and as his technology provider, Joe has been engaged in identifying, implementing and maintaining customer service solutions that are efficient, effective and promote a positive utility experience. SMECO provides power to more than 160,000 services, and its vision statement, "Putting members first," emphasizes that commitment.

CHAPTER 37

CHRIS TYRRELL
Executive Vice-President of Utility Innovation and Chief Customer Care and Conservation Officer
Toronto Hydro Corporation

Photo 37-1: Chris Tyrrell

"**T**here's no such word as can't." That saying, sometimes attributed to Henry Ford, was often used in my parents' home as I grew up. When I think back on my childhood and the ways my parents influenced me, their values and the lessons they taught, Ford's pragmatism rings in my ears. My parents were hard working and somewhat entrepreneurs, focused on work and its outcomes, often looking for something new or more, and striving to make whatever they were engaged in a success. A master electrician, my dad Jack was an engineering-type person; he worked with a variety of companies on major power projects in multiple industries. With five kids to raise, he and my mother were always looking for opportunities that could better provide for our family. My mother Barbara had a diverse career. She was a nurse, a real estate agent, a community council member, a retail store owner/operator and in her 40s she returned to college and

---

"'There's no such word as can't.'" – Chris Tyrrell

---

earned a business degree. She later became dean of the college where she eventually decided to retire. She was and remains at the age of 87 a mentor in my life, one who is extremely smart, ambitious and with an admirable, optimistic outlook on life. She believes nothing is impossible, so it's natural that "can't" wasn't part of her or my dad's lexicon.

In my professional career, four other mentors stand out. Harold Parker, Regional Manager at Ontario Hydro, took me under his wing, bringing me along and teaching me the politics germaine to the utility sector. He shared the dos and don'ts of career planning too. One axiom that I remember from our time together went something like this: "You work hard, but people will not recognize you in this big company unless you stand under the spotlight a little." We worked together for 10 years so Harold knew my responsibilities, work ethic and ambitions. I recall, after a presentation I delivered to a large audience and shadowed by other big names, he pulled me aside and made it clear that I needed to be less modest. He explained that when raising the company's profile, I should take the opportunity to raise my own to help advance my career.

Another mentor was Bob Clarkson, Area Manager at Ontario Hydro. He was my direct manager and a real inspiration, helping me understand the balance of career, family and health. Notably, he always supported me in my 10-year tenure with Ontario Hydro and promoted me through the management ranks. He inspired me to start running/jogging. Despite his disability, he jogged every day, arranging and participating in fun runs, marathons and even an ultra-marathon. He often told me that it was not only good for his disability, saying, "I have to keep moving," but explained the therapeutic and stress management benefits. I took his advice and joined him. It was not long before I was hooked and to this day, I still routinely exercise. Bob unfortunately succumbed to his disability/disease a number of years ago, but I subconsciously thank him for his mentoring every day.

"'People will not recognize you unless you stand under the spotlight a little.'" – Chris Tyrrell

---

Over the years, I count myself lucky because I've worked for some extremely good CEOs. The third mentor that stands out was Dave O'Brien, the City Manager of Mississauga when we first worked together and then as Toronto Hydro's CEO. He had an incredible way of engaging with people and led with confidence that often instilled the same in his staff and those involved. He was a pragmatic leader and had a personality a little like my father – personable and engaging, but firm and committed to getting the job done. His long successful political career/experience provided great insights to working with our shareholder, the City of Toronto. One piece of advice that jumps out at me was: "Don't underestimate the value of communications. Over communicate with those that need to understand your message." I follow that advice today, and it has no doubt helped me with effective engagement. That relationship with Dave evolved to my current CEO, Anthony Haines, a true visionary who inspires me on a regular basis. Anthony is extremely smart and has had a diverse career that brings private and public experience to a complex electricity utility industry. His calm confidence is admired, as is his strong leadership and support. He taught me the value of 'what gets measured, gets managed.' While I was always a believer of this statement, he taught me the associated strategies, plans and mechanics of driving this into the organization and its culture. Each year we outperform our past and often lead the industry in many areas.

"'What gets measured, gets managed.'" - Chris Tyrrell

If I could write a letter to any of these mentors, it would begin, "Dear Mom and Dad." Throughout my life, they helped me at every turn. My dad could do or fix just about anything, and when he coupled practical skills with his can-do attitude, that anything became possible, "can't" was banished and confidence raised. Though he passed away approximately eight years ago, I thank him every day for passing on his learnings, talents and patient guidance. I quickly get emotional when I think about my mother's influence because she's still with me today and makes me realize her unfailing optimism, unwavering values and support made me who I am. When I feel down and frustrated, she's the one I call for a listening ear, terrific advice and respect for my decisions. She is my rock.

Besides my mom, my wife Ruth has been my go-to and best friend for 37 years. Ruth and I both have careers in the utility sector, so with her firsthand knowledge, I can vent about work frustrations and the swirling political winds because she truly understands. But when we're together, she also reminds me that there's so much more we share than work. We have raised two amazing daughters that we are extremely proud of, who are married to equally amazing young men. Best of all, we are now grandparents to three incredible grandkids. Collectively, they all keep me focused on what's really important in life – my career has been important, but my family has and will always be the most important.

Toronto Hydro Corporation is a holding company which wholly owns two subsidiaries:

• Toronto Hydro-Electric System Limited (THESL), which distributes electricity and engages in conservation and demand management activities; and

• Toronto Hydro Energy Services Inc. which provides street lighting and expressway lighting services in the city of Toronto.

The principal business of the Corporation and its subsidiaries is the distribution of electricity by THESL, which owns and operates the electricity distribution system for Canada's largest city. A leader in conservation and demand management, it has 769,000 customers located in the city of Toronto and distributes approximately 19% of the electricity consumed in Ontario. Chris Tyrrell is the company's Executive Vice-President of Utility Innovation and Chief Customer Care and Conservation Officer.

CHAPTER 38

DAVE VOGEL
Executive Vice President
Louisville Water Company

Photo 38-1: Dave Vogel

When I think of someone who taught me critical lessons at a young age, I immediately think of my mother. She was born in 1935 in London, England, and immigrated to the United States when she was 19 (pretty gutsy for a single young woman in the mid-1950s). Among the many things that I learned from my mom, three of them stick out:

1. Always be on time – so you don't make others wait for you.

2. Wear clean underwear – in case you are in an accident!

3. Be polite and treat people the way you want to be treated because life is all about relationships, and you will never get anywhere in this world if you don't treat people kindly and with respect.

My mom was huge on the politeness concept (probably her English background) and drilled this into my brother, sister and me. If you

Photo 38-2: My mom

Photo 38-3: Me and my mom

wanted to really impress my mother, tell her that one of her children was very polite. When she heard this, she would just beam!

I believe that being polite can be worth hundreds of thousands of dollars, maybe more, over the course of a career. Promotions go out to those who have strong people skills and have proven they can effectively work in a team environment. You will never hear the following statement in the workplace: "Well, Dave's a real jerk and can't get along with anyone. Let's promote him!" As my mother knew, if you modelled the right behaviors, good things will come.

"Being polite can be worth hundreds of thousands of dollars, maybe more, over the course of a career."
– Dave Vogel

My first job out of college had me working as a mechanical engineer for a defense contractor in Baltimore, Maryland. I worked for a guy named George who, at the time, was is in his late 60s and obviously had several decades of work experience. George took me under his wing and let me do many things, including implementing my own designs, leading my own projects and making my own decisions. He was one of the most awesome managers I ever had.

I had been there for a couple of years, and I made a big mistake. At that time, I was still young and single, and my personal life had me going out and partying with my friends during the week (particularly on Thursday nights). On one of those occasions, I didn't make it into work until about 11 am the next day. I spent the night in a town about 30 miles away, cell phones didn't exist yet (this was the 1980s), and I didn't have easy access to a land line. When I got in, George came into my cube and was irate. I remember him looking me in the eye and pointing his finger at me stating, "Don't ever do that again!" He asked me where I was and berated me for not calling to let him know. After letting me have it for several minutes, he told me that he had been worried about my safety. He knew that I had been working on an old car at a remote family farm and thought that it may have fallen on me. He thought I might be injured with no way to reach out for help. I apologized and promised him that this would never happen again. It didn't.

"I need to lead by example." – Dave Vogel

Afterwards I realized that George wasn't upset with me because I was late. He wasn't upset with me because I didn't get work accomplished that morning. He was upset with me because he cared about me and was worried about me. He was a great person, and I would do anything for that man! So, the lessons I learned from that experience were many:

1. Be responsible.
2. Learn from your mistakes.
3. Accept feedback and get better.
4. Provide those around you feedback, so they can get better.
5. And get to know, personally, the individuals you work with. The stronger the relationships, the stronger the team.

I had just recently been promoted at a previous company. I was relatively young, and my boss at the time had a reputation of being extremely detail-oriented and a tough person to work with. I spent several years working for him, and during that time I learned a lot from him (both positive and negative) about leadership.

One year, I chaired our employee Metro United Way campaign, and my team decided to bring back a softball event that hadn't been held for a few years. Instead of an all weekend tournament which was a big commitment for our employees, we decided to do just a Friday night session and have each team play just one game.

"The person we are today has been shaped over time by all of those who have been around us." – Dave Vogel

---

There was a lot of prep work to do prior to the event, and earlier that day I shared with my boss that I would be out at the field that afternoon helping to set up. To my surprise, my manager said to me, "Does a Vice President really need to be at the field helping to set up for the game?" Without much thought, I responded, "Yes indeed, I am chairing the campaign, and I need to lead by example." The event went off without a hitch. The employees and their families loved it, and we raised a bunch of money for charity. In thinking about this experience there were a few things that I learned:

1. Trust your gut and follow your instincts.

2. Lead by example!

3. As a leader you must be involved with your team. The days of having absent leadership who feel they are above their teams is long gone.

4. You won't agree with every piece of advice you receive. The folks you work with come from all types of backgrounds and have different ideas based on their generation and work experiences.

The letter that I would write to each of these individuals would take the form of a thank you note. I once read an article on leadership which pointed out that the person we are today has been shaped over time by all of those who have been around us. The author encouraged the readers to reach out and thank those folks for the wisdom, experience and education they have passed on. So, I would like to give a big shout out and hearty thank you to all of those who have helped shape me into the person I am today.

Dave Vogel is Louisville Water's Executive Vice President. With almost one million customers, Louisville Water Company provides potable water service to residents and businesses in Louisville Metro and parts of Bullitt, Hardin, Nelson, Oldham, Shelby and Spencer counties.

CHAPTER 39

MARGARET WRIGHT
Assistant Director, 311 Customer Service Center
City of Dallas

Photo 39-1: Margaret Wright

Well, I never thought of my parents as "mentors," but the principles that have influenced my work came from them. They were young adults in the Depression, and my father's parents were Finnish immigrants. He was the only one in his family to graduate from college. There is a Finnish word "sisu" that means "grit" or "spunk," and he both valued and demonstrated that quality.

I saw my parents work hard. One of my dad's favorite admonitions to his children and grandchildren was, "Keep your head down and your fanny up," a variation on keeping your nose to the grindstone. And yet, they set aside time away from work for relaxation. I learned that, for me, putting work above everything else in my life was not a workable route.

"If you said you are going to do something, do it."
— Margaret Wright

193

Photo 39-2: My parents

My parents also stressed keeping commitments. If you said you were going to do something, do it. Self-sufficiency was important and so was not thinking you were too good to pitch in to get a job done. In short, many of the traits that got them through hard times became living lessons to me and my siblings, even though we didn't realize it at the time.

I've spent the majority of my working life in the public sector, where every decision, email, action, etc., is subject to public scrutiny, including providing access to documents under the Freedom of Information Act. So, following policies and being careful about what precedent is set in various actions are important guideposts (the words to Carly Simon's song, "We Have No Secrets," frequently run through my head).

> **"'Policies are created to address routine situations, but special circumstances call for more evaluation and perhaps a deviation from policy.'" – Margaret Wright**

However, a wise manager at my city once commented, "Policies are created to address routine situations, but special circumstances call for more evaluation and perhaps a deviation from the policy." I have thought often about that lesson, and it has helped me confidently handle unusual situations. If I'm doing something "non-standard," do I have good justification? Can I defend why I didn't follow policy "to a T" (because, remember, we have no secrets)?

There was a fast-rising executive in an organization where I worked that, to be generous, left a lot of collateral damage in his wake. He was rumored to have the ear of the chief executive, and several lower-level staff sought his advice or patronage in hopes of moving up in the organization under his wing. He ran roughshod over people, disregarded policy, was dismissive of staff that didn't suck up to him, yet he framed his actions as decisive and impactful. By challenging the status quo, he wanted his boss and others to see him as a change agent.

About the same time, Robert Sutton, a professor at Stanford, published a book titled, *The No Asshole Rule*. The book described the bullying behavior I saw in the executive, and it confirmed for me that there was nothing about his style that I admired or wanted to emulate. Years later, after the chief executive retired, the new CEO sidelined the bully to a completely isolated and useless role, and after a couple of years he was laid off. Not sure anyone was sorry to see him go.

Bullying behavior is not to be admired or emulated.
– Margaret Wright

I have stayed in touch with the wise manager mentor (who also ended up being my boss a few years later). I have reminded him several times of that sage advice, and he laughingly claims to have no memory of having said it! So perhaps the message there is that you never know what wisdom (or stupidity!) will stick with people.

Margaret Wright is the Assistant Director, 311 Customer Service Center for the City of Dallas, the ninth largest city in the U.S. 311 provides access to City services 24 hours a day, 7 days a week for routine calls as well as urgent requests such as street leaks, burst pipes, sewer issues, sick, confined or injured animals, animal bites, traffic signal outages, downed signal light poles, street spillages and downed trees. 311 is the call center for Dallas Water Utilities, providing round the clock service request initiation, field dispatching, customer contact and service information.

CHAPTER 40

MARK WYATT
Vice President (Retired)
Duke Energy

Photo 40-1: Mark Wyatt

My dad introduced me to the manager of a local movie theater where we lived when I became old enough to receive a work permit. The manager's name was Berlyn Edward Smiley; he was best known as "B.E." to those who knew him well. Mr. Smiley, which I always respectfully called him, gave me my first job working in the theater. I started working as a concession stand attendant and eventually graduated to ticket taker, and several years later was promoted to assistant manager. The job taught me a lot about working with the public, and what impressed me most was the passion Mr. Smiley displayed when it came to serving movie goers. He was quick to point out when it was time to stock the candy case or put out a fresh batch of popcorn. Customers should never have to ask for something; what they want should always be readily available. I worked at the theater throughout my middle and high school years and was fortunate enough to have the opportunity to work during holidays and over the summer when I was home from college. The two biggest lessons I learned from working for Mr. Smiley were

Photo 40-2: B. E. Smiley, my early mentor at the movie theater

"Always treat your customers the way you would want to be treated," and "You need to have faith and trust in your workers to do their job." It was fun and rewarding to see movie goers walk away with a smile after serving them candy, popcorn or a drink. It was equally rewarding for me to earn the faith and confidence of Mr. Smiley to do my job, as he rewarded me throughout the years with increasing levels of responsibility. Even when I made a mistake, he was quick to support and coach me on what I could do to prevent it from happening again – never a demeaning word was said, even when I screwed up the most!

> "'Always treat your customers the way you would want to
> be treated,' and 'You need to have faith and trust in your
> workers to do their job.'" – Mark Wyatt

There are two individuals who made a significant impact on me both personally and professionally during my business career. The first person I would like to talk about is Ruth Shaw, who at the time I worked for her was the President of Duke Power Company. Ruth was one of the most outgoing, driven, highly-respected business leaders I have had the privilege to work for. Ruth had an infectious passion for her employees and an equally infectious passion for serving customers of the company. Every opportunity she got, she would spend time with employees, from all hands meetings where no questions were off limits to having lunch in the company cafeteria with one or more employees. She always spent a significant amount of her time in the field meeting with customers to hear their concerns and needs as well as taking the opportunity to educate them on company and industry direction, challenges and opportunities. We received some of the highest customer satisfaction ratings ever during Ruth's tenure as President, and I firmly believe Ruth played a huge role in helping the company achieve these ratings through her active engagement with our customers.

> "Always respect and trust your employees. By providing
> them with the right tools and guidance, the rest will take
> care of itself." – Mark Wyatt

The second person I would like to talk about is Gianna Manes, who at the time I worked for her was Senior Vice President and Chief Customer

Photo 40-3: Gianna Manes, former Duke Energy SVP and CCO, now President and CEO of ENMAX

Officer of Duke Energy. Gianna was one of the most energetic, optimistic and fun-loving leaders I have worked for. She lit up the room when she walked in, regardless of whether it was in a one-on-one setting or a larger gathering. She was truly interested in knowing more about you as a person and always led off the conversation with this in mind. She was a visionary, always looking for and seeing what was possible. She believes employees are the lifeblood of an organization's success. To that end, she was never hesitant to promote or place someone in a role of increasing responsibility for them to grow and contribute at the next level.

Both Ruth and Gianna taught me the value of listening to, grooming and providing growth opportunities for employees, since they are truly the lifeblood of any company's ability to prosper and grow. They both had an incredible belief and expectation that you should always question every business decision to ensure that it either directly or indirectly benefits the end customer of the company. If it didn't, it should not be done.

The key lessons I learned from working for both leaders were to always respect and trust your employees. By providing them with the right tools and guidance, the rest will take care of itself. Additionally, always focus on the reason your organization or company exists – to serve the end customer. They should always be factored into all business decisions you make.

"Take time for yourself, your family and your friends."
– Mark Wyatt

I have had the privilege of knowing or working with many individuals whom I did not really consider mentors at the time we got to know each other or when we worked together. As time has passed, I have come to appreciate the value of these relationships and the subtle (and not so subtle!) things I have come to realize were valuable lessons learned. There are two lessons I would like to discuss from these relationships. The first is: Take time for yourself, your family and your friends. Some of the best personal relationships I have exist because we both recognize it is okay to slow down and enjoy the moment or each other's company. I have observed many times where individuals do not do this because they prioritize higher some other aspect of their life, usually work, and they find out after it is too late that you have lost or eroded a valuable friend or relationship. The second is: Always do what you say you are going to do, and if not, please let the other person know you are not able to do it. This has happened to me on numerous occasions, mostly in the business world. Great, well-intentioned individuals who I dearly respect did not follow through on this simple principle. Credibility, trust and respect can be quickly lost if this becomes a pattern in life.

Dear Gianna, Ruth, and Mr. Smiley:

Now that I have entered the next phase of life, retirement, I have come to appreciate more the many blessings life has given me. I would like to thank each of you for the privilege of getting to know you, and more importantly, getting the opportunity to learn from you. As each of you know from working with me, I enjoy having the freedom to grow, learn and try new things. You were willing to give me the opportunities necessary to do the things I enjoyed most and were equally patient with me as I tried knew things, including those things that did not always work out for the best! You encouraged me, supported me and provided invaluable guidance throughout our time together. You further strengthened my belief that, if you treat your employees well, coach them, encourage them and give them space to grow, the sky is the limit! You also helped me realize that getting to know an individual personally is one of the greatest gifts you can give as well as receive.

Thanks for all you have done to help me appreciate and value the many lessons you have taught me.

Mark Wyatt retired from Duke Energy in 2013 with 34 years of senior management and utility experience. Prior to his retirement, Mark served as Vice President of Grid Modernization where he was the lead executive for the company's grid modernization function and accountable for delivering enhanced operational efficiencies for the company's transmission and distribution system, as well as providing a platform for growing the company's revenue through leveraging grid modernization investments to provide value-added products and services to the company's retail customer base. Duke Energy provides electricity to 7.6 million customers in six states.

CHAPTER 41

SUMMARY

Reflecting on the 2,000 plus years of experience shared on the pages of this book, there are so many leadership lessons to be gleaned – lessons on how to build trust while fostering the future, solutions, strategy, planning, motivation, excellence, success, quality and innovation, traits that characterize successful organizations everywhere, including utilities. These lessons are not technical in nature. Rather, they are guidelines to follow as you develop and shape your most important asset – people.

These lessons can be deployed immediately. I would encourage you to build these lessons into your everyday interactions with people. You will see remarkable results in all walks of your life as you incorporate the values shared within these pages with everyone you encounter, be it your immediate family members, staff or volunteers.

> "Treat others the way you would like to be treated, especially if you're the boss." – David J. McKendry

As you see progress, make some notes and reflect on the lessons you have learned, both from this book and from your own key influencers.

I have so appreciated the incredible wisdom that the co-authors of *Leadership Lessons Learned from Our Mentors* have shared. I have learned so much as I hope you have. They have shown that leadership is not about being the best. Leadership is about making everyone else better. Leadership is about lifting up those around you.

If I were to try and summarize all the lessons so willingly offered into one sentence, I think it would boil down to this: abide by the Golden Rule. Treat others the way you would like to be treated, especially if you're the boss. To be a successful leader, it all comes down to people and building trust by treating them with dignity, respect, appreciation, recognition, value and worth.

Thank you for taking the time to learn from these accomplished, remarkable leaders and the lessons their mentors have poured into each of them. Collectively, it is our hope that the lessons we have learned will be of value to you as the torch is passed to the next generation of leaders who will continue to shape the utility customer experience of the future.

Best wishes,
Dave

AUTHOR'S BIOGRAPHY

As Senior Fellow with the Canadian Electricity Association, David J. McKendry is a respected, customer-focused, action-oriented business leader. With over 35 years of domestic and international utility experience in the electricity, telecommunications and high-tech sectors, including over 15 years with Hydro Ottawa where he served as Director Customer Service, McKendry possesses a wide range of strengths in the areas of Customer Service, Marketing, Sales, Communications, Conservation and Demand Management and Business Development.

He has championed many industry-leading initiatives benefitting both the customer and the utility.

He is a past Chair of the Canadian Electricity Association's Customer Council, sits on the Board of Directors of CS Week, one of the largest utility customer service conferences in North America, and is an often-requested speaker at industry events. McKendry is featured as one of eight leading North American utility "all-stars" in Penni McLean-Conner's 2016 book, *Profiles in Excellence: Utility Chief Customer Officers.*

A graduate of Carleton University (B.A.), McKendry also holds a Masters Certificate in Energy Sector Leadership from York University in Toronto.

McKendry serves in a number of capacities within the not-for-profit sector and is a member of United Way Ottawa's Revenue Committee.

APPENDIX A: PHOTOS

CHAPTER 1: DAVID J. MCKENDRY

Photo 1-1: David J. McKendry

Photo 1-2: Felicity McKendry, my mother

Photo 1-3: Spence McKendry, my father

Photo 1-4: James Howard Bennett, my grandfather

Photo 1-5: Louie Nozzolillo, my uncle

Photo 1-6: Connie Nozzolillo, my aunt

Photo 1-7: My uncle Wilmot Young and me

Photo 1-8: Pat O'Brien, my basketball coach at Carleton University

Photo 1-9: Arden Brooks, my boss at Canadian Tire

Photo 1-10: Ray Byrne (back row, far right), my boss at Bell Canada and one of the best bosses ever

Photo 1-11: Don Bertrand, my dad's boss and mentor

CHAPTER 2: TODD ARNOLD

Photo 2-1: Todd Arnold

Photo 2-2: Arnold's Newsstand, Sullivan, IN

CHAPTER 3: FRANCIS BRADLEY

Photo 3-1: Francis Bradley

CHAPTER 4: SANDRA BROUGHTON

Photo 4-1: Sandra Broughton
Photo 4-2: My grandmothers Nellie and Carrie with my mother Julia in
          1972
Photo 4-3: Julia, my mother
Photo 4-4: My family
Photo 4-5: One of my earliest professional mentors, Fredric A. Stanley
Photo 4-6: Another one of my career influencers, Grover Thomas
Photo 4-7: My best friend Paula E. Bonds

CHAPTER 5: LISA CAGNOLATTI

Photo 5-1: Lisa Cagnolatti
Photo 5-2: My mother, Jeri Cagnolatti
Photo 5-3: Carolyn Green, my early mentor at Southern California Gas
          Company
Photo 5-4: Dick Rosenblum, my sounding board at Southern California
          Edison

CHAPTER 6: EILEEN CAMPBELL

Photo 6-1: Eileen Campbell
Photo 6-2: My dad Albert Campbell and me
Photo 6-3: Max Cananzi, one of my greatest career influencers

CHAPTER 7: CHRIS CARDENAS

Photo 7-1: Chris Cardenas

CHAPTER 8: ELLIS CHANDLEE

Photo 8-1: Ellis Chandlee
Photo 8-2: Me, retired and relaxed by the pool

CHAPTER 9: CHIMAOBI CHIJIOKE

Photo 9-1: Chimaobi Chijioke
Photo 9-2: Morlon Bell-Izzard, a key mentor

CHAPTER 21: JULIE LUPINACCI

Photo 21-1: Julie Lupinacci
Photo 21:2: My mom and dad, John and Germaine Gaudet
Photo 21-3: Mom and me in the car with sunrise or sunset in the
      windshield
Photo 21-4: My mass book photo
Photo 21-5: My husband Claudio and me

CHAPTER 22: CONNIE MCINTYRE

Photo 22-1: Connie McIntyre
Photo 22-2: Me and my dad on my wedding day
Photo 22-3: My mentor Hank Linginfelter, a "big picture guy"
Photo 22-4: Catherine Land-Waters, my mentor who taught me to have
      a voice
Photo 22-5: Bryan Batson, another key career mentor

CHAPTER 23: PENNI MCLEAN-CONNER

Photo 23-1: Penni McLean-Conner

CHAPTER 24: CECIL MCMASTER

Photo 24-1: Cecil McMaster

CHAPTER 25: KERRY OVERTON

Photo 25-1: Kerry Overton
Photo 25-2: Hardy Overton, Sr., my dad
Photo 25-3: My mother, Betty Overton
Photo 25-4: My pastor, the Reverend Joseph C. Parker, Jr.

CHAPTER 26: ANDREA PELT-THORNTON

Photo 26-1: Andrea Pelt-Thornton

CHAPTER 27: BECKY POPE

Photo 27-1: Becky Pope

Photo 27-2: George Reel, my mentor and GUC's Director of Customer
Relations

Photo 27-3: Me and Sandy Barnes, GUC's Director of Information
Technology

CHAPTER 28: HALLIE REESE

Photo 28-1: Hallie Reese

Photo 28-2: Lee Chappine, my high school softball coach

Photo 28-3: Family photo with my grandfather, Dan Salerno

CHAPTER 29: KIM RICH

Photo 29-1: Kim Rich

Photo 29-2: My grandmothers Carolyn Allen, Grace Lindsey and Audrey
Brock and me, May 1993

Photo 29-3: Grandma Allen, me, Grandma Brock and my sister Kristi
Cater, January 2010

Photo 29-4: My sister Kristi, Grandma Lindsey and me, August 2010

CHAPTER 30: VINAY SHARMA

Photo 30-1: Vinay Sharma

CHAPTER 31: BILL SHEPHERD

Photo 31-1: Bill Shepherd

Photo 31-2: Coach Wright, my high school football coach

Photo 31-3: Kathy Viehe, my boss and then Interim General Manager at
GRU

CHAPTER 32: TONY SIMAS

Photo 32-1: Tony Simas

Photo 32-2: My father, Jose Simas

Photo 32-3: My daughter, Danielle

Photo 32-4: Archie Christopher (Chris), my early mentor

Photo 32-5: My mentor Jonathan Carey, manager of customer care at
Commonwealth Gas

CHAPTER 33: KAREN SPARKMAN

Photo 33-1: Karen Sparkman

Photo 33-2: My mother Annamaria and me

CHAPTER 34: JERRY SULLIVAN

Photo 34-1: Jerry Sullivan

Photo 34-2: Father Anton J. Renna, S.J., my teacher and mentor

Photo 34-3: U.S. Military Academy - West Point, Class of 1976 Cadet Company: F2

Photo 34-4: General of the Army Omar Bradley, my mentor who spoke about 10 leadership principles

Photo 34-5: Brigadier General John Jannarone, my mentor who saw a succession planning gap at Consolidated Edison

Photo 34-6: Dr. Joyce Orsini, Deming's graduate assistant and one of my mentors

CHAPTER 35: DAVE TOMLINSON

Photo 35-1: Dave Tomlinson

CHAPTER 36: JOE TRENTACOSTA

Photo 36-1: Joe Trentacosta

Photo 36-2: Me with a yo-yo, sister Rosemarie and Grandpa at Grandpa Ro Joe Chicken Market

Photo 36-3: Mom and Dad (in his NYPD uniform)

CHAPTER 37: CHRIS TYRRELL

Photo 37-1: Chris Tyrrell

CHAPTER 38: DAVE VOGEL

Photo 38-1: Dave Vogel

Photo 38-2: My mom

Photo 38-3: Me and my mom

CHAPTER 39: MARGARET WRIGHT

Photo 39-1: Margaret Wright

Photo 39-2: My parents

CHAPTER 40: MARK WYATT

Photo 40-1: Mark Wyatt

Photo 40-2: B. E. Smiley, my early mentor at the movie theater

Photo 40-3: Gianna Manes, former Duke Energy SVP and CCO, now
                President and CEO of ENMAX

APPENDIX B:
LEADERSHIP LESSONS LEARNED
REFERENCE GUIDE

I have taken the liberty of selecting some of the key takeaways shared in this book (470 in fact). A few have been repeated purposely as they were mentioned separately by different authors. I have paraphrased them into this "reference guide," a list that can be used as a compass to ensure that your leadership journey remains on course. I hope you find this reference guide helpful.

470 LEADERSHIP LESSONS LEARNED

1. Be an encourager; be a positive influence.

2. "Keep the top half of the tank full."

3. Visualize the steps to be taken.

4. If a job is worth doing, it's worth doing right.

5. Treat other people's property with respect. Leave things better than you found them.

6. Do the right thing.

7. Remember the value of service and sacrifice.

8. Walk softly and garner respect not by the power of your position but by the conduct of your character.

9. Continually challenge your team in a very encouraging way.

10. Treat others the way you would like to be treated, especially if you're the boss.

11. Jointly determine and get buy-in to what needs to be done.

12. Give the rope necessary, which can be pulled either way - but don't use the rope to micro-manage.

13. Celebrate success and give credit to the team.

14. Laugh along the way.

15. Don't take yourself too seriously.

16. Use the power of MBWA – Management By Walking Around.

17. Continually ask yourself: do I personally have to do this, or can it be delegated? Delegate everything you can.

18. Plan the work, work the plan.

19. Remember the power of the handwritten note sent to the employee's home.

20. You can't manage what you can't measure.

21. Start with the end in mind and put it into pictures so people can visualize the goal.

22. It's not about looks; it's about substance.

23. It's not about win/lose; it's about win/win.

24. People don't leave jobs; they leave their bosses.

25. "Train people well enough so that they can leave, treat them well enough so that they don't want to."

26. Equip others so they can be all they can be.

27. Do what you say you are going to do.

28. Show up on time.

29. Communicate the good, the bad, the ugly.

30. Don't let things fester. Fess up.

31. The truth is always the best path to take. Don't lie. It is never the best path. Full stop.

32. Say please and thank you.

33. Honey will get you further than vinegar.

34. "Be tough on the issues and easy on the people."

35. Hold regular meetings with staff and ask for their input.

36. Help others get what they want, and they will help you get what you want.

37. "People don't care how much you know until they know how much you care."

38. Don't respond in haste. Sleep on it.

39. Be humble.

40. Be thankful.

41. Listen.

42. Be genuine.

43. Use three powerful words, "Help me understand…"

44. The most important question that a leader can ask is, "How can I help?"

45. If people didn't make mistakes, pencils wouldn't need erasers.

46. Praise in public, discipline in private.

47. Give the credit and take the blame.

48. Catch people doing things right.

49. Don't be afraid to step forward to make things better.

50. Lead from where you are.

51. Don't get discouraged as you take on leadership roles.

52. Practice left foot, right foot – because sometimes it is just head down slow steady progress that gets things done.

53. People are like string; don't push them, lead instead and they will follow.

54. It's not the hard skills and soft skills; it is the hard skills and the harder skills.

55. Exceed customer expectations one customer at a time.

56. Open-ended questions foster innovation.

57. Be mindful of voice and posture.

58. Read books and literature.

59. Mentorship lessons reach across generations.

60. Stand by your team, and they will stand by you.

61. Let people know how much you appreciate them in the living years.

62. It is not only **what** you do in a leadership role, but **how** you do it.

63. An enthusiastic, can-do attitude is contagious.

64. The customer is always right.

65. Greet customers with a smile and never forget to say thank you.

66. Find times in your career to serve your customers directly.

67. Find people with potential and give them opportunities to grow and excel.

68. A great leader must make tough decisions that won't make everyone happy.

69. Great careers, even when working for the greatest of mentors, are not linear.

70. Discover the most undervalued mentors – books.

71. Find joy in all things.

72. Teachers play an enormous role in the lives of their students.

73. Everyone has a story, and everyone's stories are different.

74. While words are meaningful, they are made more so when backed by action.

75. See the power of people behind an idea.

76. You can't appreciate others' "wants" until you have walked in their shoes.

77. Spend time with customers and get to know them.

78. Read books.

79. Dream.

80. Learn as much as you can.

81. You can do and be anything you want to do and be.

82. Persevere, learn from mistakes, adjust the plan, get the results you want.

83. Be humble, kind, resourceful and reconciling.

84. Sit side by side; coach until the concept is mastered or at a minimum understood.

85. Take calculated risks.

86. Ask for others' opinions. Build trust by accepting others' positions.

87. Teach and coach through storytelling and self-deprecating humor.

88. Never limit yourself.

89. Know your value.

90. Don't shy away from being challenged ethically, intellectually, morally and socially.

91. Ensure stakeholder engagement early and remove barriers to success.

92. Silence can be misinterpreted. Add your voice to the conversation and be authentic with your views.

93. Be self-aware of your behavior, image and interpersonal interactions.

94. Learn something different to accelerate your professional development.

95. Growth only happens when you push yourself outside your comfort zone.

96. Behave like a superstar no matter your work assignment because that's who you are.

97. You are always on stage as a leader, and everything you do and say matters.

98. No matter how people behave or treat you, never let it change who you are.

99. Work hard, work smart, treat everyone with respect.

100. Know employee's names and those of their children.

101. There is power in relationships.

102. Value everyone's contributions.

103. Believe in yourself.

104. Don't distance yourself from the front line.

105. Surround yourself with great people and promote from within.

106. Take on greater leadership roles outside of your job.

107. Actions speak louder than words.

108. Foster an environment that is supportive, open and transparent to achieve an engaged workforce.

109. Being successful takes perseverance and determination.

110. No personal growth comes from taking the easy road.

111. Value and appreciate others regardless of the job they perform.

112. Respect others, work hard, deliver a quality product.

113. Be authentic.

114. Knowing and playing the political game is critical.

115. View leadership as a privilege, not a divine right.

116. Once your team understands your core values and trusts you have their best interest at heart, they'll follow anywhere and do anything for you.

117. Get to know your staff and develop relationships to build trust and respect.

118. Never neglect the frontline workers who do the heavy lifting.

119. A job worth doing is worth doing well.

120. Understanding the underlying business issue allows you to construct a better mousetrap.

121. Don't be all stick and no carrot.

122. Set people up for success by setting realistic goals and reward performance.

123. Appreciate and recognize ideas.

124. Care for people by teaching them how to be successful.

125. Correction is for betterment, not punishment.

126. Be calm under pressure regardless of the situation.

127. Be confident and calm for your team.

128. Don't dwell on the problems; focus on the solutions.

129. Help staff understand the rationale behind decisions, policies and procedures.

130. Be on time.

131. Don't run away when you are angry.

132. Take time to refuel.

133. Be accountable.

134. Have integrity.

135. Show respect.

136. Give honest, direct feedback privately and as near-time as possible.

137. When complimenting work, be specific and precise with words, and don't use "but."

138. Action speaks louder than words, but not nearly as often.

139. Value volunteerism.

140. Include others.

141. Develop cross-organizational teams.

142. Know your stuff.

143. Prepare in advance.

144. Often the greatest lessons are taught by those who do not know they are teaching.

145. Consider how you influence what your team relates to their families at their dinner tables.

146. Foster positive experiences.

147. Focus on removing obstacles.

148. Make jobs easier rather than harder.

149. Measure your success through other's success.

150. Never underestimate how much influence you have.

151. Never underestimate how fleeting time can be.

152. Let people learn things in their own way.

153. To build trust, one must feel recognized, included, respected and their self-esteem preserved.

154. Consider the importance of constructive, frank and honest discussion when evaluating strategies and examining potential upsides and downside.

155. Understand risk and safety.

156. Keep learning and encourage creativity and learning.

157. Get organized and, when chaos comes, stay calm.

158. Make good use of what you already have.

159. Listen to the customer.

160. Offer and reach a fair exchange of value.

161. Learn from everyone.

162. Always respect, refer to and recognize others.

163. Find stuff that makes a difference, and plan and measure results.

164. Think about the impact on everyone and everything, especially customers, co-workers and shareholders.

165. Little changes add up to a lot.

166. Stay in good humor.

167. Listen to stories and use stories to improve communication.

168. Share knowledge, and you will receive more than your share back.

169. Take measured risks, make mistakes and laugh at them.

170. Celebrate success.

171. Create and support fun time with your family and friends.

172. Be enthusiastic, but if you need to borrow resources, be sure to ask first.

173. Connection between people creates strong teams and effective leaders.

174. To get from point A to point B, don't always expect to go in a straight line.

175. Sometimes taking longer makes for a smoother transition and easier adoption.

176. Create an environment where people are focused on the customer.

177. Career success is about enjoying what you do every day at work.

178. Present all the facts whether they support your position or not.

179. Credibility and trust can take a lifetime to learn but can be lost in a few words or with no words at all.

180. Praise in public and punish in private.

181. Catch people doing things right.

182. Document your goals.

183. Do things the right way for the benefit of customers, the company and the employees.

184. Give people a second chance.

185. Be honest.

186. Operate with integrity.

187. Live within your means.

188. Avoid paralysis by analysis.

189. If you enjoy your job, you'll never work a day in your life.

190. Have an open mind and listen to seek understanding.

191. Be proud of your work ethic.

192. Be a great teammate.

193. Encourage others and recognize them for things done well.

194. Be willing to try things you don't like.

195. Focus on improving support to those around you.

196. Ensure that clear expectations are set and that all agree.

197. Listen and provide guidance without giving direction.

198. Look to data to help identify the root cause of issues.

199. Reach out to peers to help work through challenges.

200. Focus on the people and the customer.

201. Let people learn from your mistakes.

202. Listen to customers.

203. Work hard to correct mistakes when they occur. Work even harder to prevent mistakes from occurring in the first place.

204. Learn to play all the positions on the court.

205. Continue to develop through mentoring relationships.

206. Leave it better than you found it.

207. Instill a love of learning.

208. Reading is essential for success.

209. Reinforce the importance of education every day.

210. Pursue excellence in all you do.

211. Always define the problem, organize the work, care about the people and pay attention to detail.

212. Face adversity and maintain your dignity.

213. Take pride in your work.

214. Be fearless and do not be intimidated by anyone.

215. Just because you're poor doesn't mean you have to have an impoverished mind.

216. Appreciate the sustaining energy generated by a cohesive, loving family and pride of family heritage.

217. Respect others.

218. Appreciate diversity in thought.

219. Value perseverance, hard work, thoughtfulness and humility.

220. Recognize the importance of education and life-long learning.

221. Believe in yourself.

222. Trust your judgment and instincts.

223. Find balance in both work and personal life.

224. Understand the power of a written vision statement.

225. Pace yourself when changing culture, systems and processes. You are running a marathon rather than a continuous series of sprints.

226. Take small bites at the apple.

227. Make smaller organizations within an organization and set them up to be successful.

228. Success will follow when a vision is set, parameters of success have been communicated and people are given permission to fail.

229. Provide a safe environment to think and perform outside the box.

230. Don't fall in love with processes.

231. Celebrate success along the way.

232. It's not about you; it is about the people that are brave enough to follow and execute on an idea, concept or plan.

233. Success is not your own; it is a culmination of experience, relationships and circumstance.

234. You are the driver of your life.

235. You can achieve more than you know.

236. You deserve everything you hope and dream for.

237. Go out and get it!

238. To gain traction on change initiatives, start from where others are standing and don't rush thinking.

239. People are complex. Know where they are coming from.

240. When team members understand that actions being implemented encompass their thoughts, processes and views, it leads to a higher level of engagement.

241. Demonstrate a strong work ethic.

242. Ensure a clear sense that you are doing the right things.

243. Realize the importance of being honest in what you do and say.

244. Finish what you start. If you say you're going to do something, then follow through.

245. Try new things.

246. Look at situations through different angles and understand the impacts from all sides.

247. Roll up your sleeves, do some research, ask experts for advice, don't get defensive.

248. Speak up.

249. There is no such thing as "I can't."

250. Even the most obvious things can be obscured by one's perceptions, filters and personal biases.

251. Take the time to understand people's professional goals and ambitions.

252. Provide opportunities.

253. Listen, walk in your customer's shoes, understand their issues and appreciate what they truly want or need.

254. Books, webinars and conferences provide best practices, philosophies, methodologies and alternate management techniques.

255. Know when to stop and move on.

256. Find a support system that can celebrate with you, lift you up, dust you off and set you straight.

257. Listen to understand.

258. Respect others.

259. Be humble.

260. Be vulnerable.

261. Have a yearn to learn.

262. Maintain your integrity.

263. Connect the dots.

264. Know your audience.

265. Bloom where you are planted.

266. Major on the majors, but know the devil is in the detail.

267. Realize the importance of living and playing and stopping to smell the roses along the way.

268. You can't just have ideas or dreams; you must share them.

269. You can't just speak; you must speak up.

270. Public speaking helps gain confidence, and with confidence, collaboration and leadership.

271. Demonstrate care and empathy for employees.

272. Know your employees' names and their goals.

273. Use stories to explain business concepts.

274. To provide great care to customers, you must first provide great care to employees.

275. Be true to yourself.

276. Truly care for your employees.

277. Commit to your team. Care intensely about their well-being. Desire that they be successful with their jobs and projects.

278. Listen carefully to what is being said or asked.

279. Keep learning all the time.

280. Take time off to refresh and enjoy time away from work.

281. Be an encourager, provide support, be positive.

282. Love and be disciplined.

283. Value hard work, service, respect for others, responsibility, confidence and unity.

284. Display a pleasant demeanor.

285. Solve problems without driving dissention. Maintain respect for everyone involved.

286. Don't shy away from conflict. Instead, go to great lengths to ensure people's well-being and spirits are taken care of in a positive way.

287. Model a sense of duty, respect for community and graciousness.

288. Provide structure and continuity.

289. Commit to helping others.

290. Work hard; treat people well.

291. Reach success on the principle that there's more that all of us can achieve together.

292. Don't eliminate, oppress or suppress others.

293. Take responsibility for your actions and words and the way they influence others.

294. Stay positive, be encouraging and support people whenever and wherever.

295. Value diversity.

296. Be responsible and consistent.

297. Be ready; be prepared both mentally and physically to rise to the challenge.

298. Change doubt into determination.

299. Believe in the plan and execute together.

300. Influence teammates to accept personal responsibility.

301. A strong work ethic and delivery will win trust.

302. Think it through, look at the big picture, engage others when tackling multiple tasks.

303. Pay attention to the details.

304. Develop a schematic in your mind. Look for what-if scenarios and plan for contingencies.

305. Take calculated risks.

306. Operate with integrity.

307. Demonstrate accountability to individuals and meet their customized needs.

308. Stay balanced; see the weighty and the important as well as the humor.

309. Muster the courage to be the best we each can be.

310. Understand who you are and that is good enough.

311. Set goals and work the plan.

312. With determination, hard work, encouragement and support, the possibilities are great.

313. Accept people for who they are and start from the place of their own significance.

314. Encourage, be positive, stay supportive.

315. Find balance, set goals, compete when the stakes are high.

316. What you put in directly influences the outcome and what you get out of it.

317. Remain humble.

318. Be nice.

319. Be fair.

320. Take risks even when dealing with some unknowns.

321. Operate with others' interests in mind.

322. It's all about the work and the effort.

323. Stand up, avoid self-pity and be confident, even in intimidating circumstances.

324. Stand by your word and stand by your team members as they are the keys to success.

325. Stick to your principles.

326. Be forthright with business partners, even if they might not like what you have to say.

327. Treat people with respect, be honest and committed to doing the right thing.

328. It's ok to speak softly while being a heavy weight by knowing your stuff.

329. Follow your heart, gut and history.

330. Utilize different philosophies or styles.

331. Practice "Boots on the Ground Leadership." Get in the trenches and work with your team.

332. Have an open-door policy.

333. Be honest.

334. Trust others.

335. Have nothing but the best in mind for people.

336. Good communication by all leaders at all levels of the organization is important to success.

337. 100% of the problems are known on the front line or in the trenches, so listen closely there.

338. There is absolutely no substitution for paying attention to the details.

339. Anticipate situations you will encounter and prepare to face them.

340. It's okay to admit when you are wrong.

341. Don't lie. It's only your word and integrity that you have at the end of the day.

342. Reach high and think big.

343. Ask questions and let the team answer. They usually figure out what needs to happen and what steps to take.

344. Pick a mood.

345. Take one day at a time.

346. To gain power, you have to give up power.

347. As a leader you cast a very long shadow. Everyone is watching.

348. Value the uniqueness of each individual's personality, skills, tastes and foibles.

349. Relationships are built through a shared journey, comradery and humor.

350. Remember the power of an inspirational hand-written card.

351. Develop an environment that fosters a solid work ethic and commitment and rewards jobs well done.

352. Find areas for opportunity and improvement.

353. Initiate projects and drive them to completion.

354. Invest in people.

355. Know and share how the company produces revenue and how each person impacts the bottom line.

356. Develop an enterprise mindset; see the big picture and communicate how each person fits in.

357. Get your hands dirty. Show that you are willing and able to learn other's duties.

358. Walk the walk and talk the talk.

359. Proactively take responsibility for your own path.

360. Learn.

361. Step up to leadership roles.

362. It's okay to say no.

363. Just because a decision is hard doesn't make the decision wrong.

364. Demonstrate resiliency, dedication and hard work.

365. Identifying and solving problems are hallmarks of great leaders.

366. Do the work, stay on task, complete assignments.

367. Lead by stepping aside or pushing others forward.

368. Practice kindness, honesty and a complete lack of pretension or need for recognition.

369. Remember the importance of connecting with others.

370. Leadership is relationship. Show humility, hold up a servant-like attitude, relate to others openly and honestly and break down not build up barriers.

371. Practice tenacity, selflessness, staying connected and engagement with others.

372. Value hard work, diligence and practice.

373. Roll up your sleeves, go shoulder to shoulder and be part of the unit.

374. Value humility, employee engagement and navigating the local political climate.

375. You cannot make any assumptions that others know your abilities. You must always be ready to sell your abilities.

376. Praise publicly and criticize privately.

377. Don't snub ideas or viewpoints.

378. Great leaders surround themselves with folks who are smarter than they are.

379. Break down barriers.

380. Lead by example.

381. Be respectful.

382. Be inclusive.

383. Live life to the fullest.

384. Value diversity.

385. Show sincere concern.

386. Promote collaboration.

387. Show consideration.

388. Be accessible.

389. See the possibilities not the abilities.

390. Don't take things for granted.

391. Life is too short.

392. Be kind to others.

393. Take the time to understand differing perspectives.

394. Look at life through diverse lenses without applying judgment.

395. Life isn't always fair.

396. There will be times when the outcome is beyond our control. When this happens, make the best of the situation.

397. Value people.

398. Look at failure as an opportunity to grow, learn or do better next time.

399. Put other's success in front of your own.

400. Use your strengths to fill the gaps in others.

401. Assign stretch goals and then provide guidance and help.

402. Inspire others and help them grow and flourish in their own right.

403. Build teams with diverse backgrounds.

404. Believe in yourself even when you are struggling to believe in yourself.

405. Mentors add spark and inspire continued learning, a desire to understand more and make a difference in life.

406. Mentors can come from all around you.

407. Find your best traits and use them.

408. Make everyone feel important, listen to every issue, take action on things that matter.

409. Do your homework.

410. Value a culture of measurement, outcomes, analysis and fact-based management.

411. Treat the customer fairly and provide honest value.

412. Learn both academically and by getting personally involved with the work.

413. Always have time for your employees.

414. When thinking "someone should do something about…" – that someone is you.

415. Don't focus on where you spent your time; instead, communicate what you changed or accomplished.

416. Form personal relationships with staff.

417. Use humor to lighten the mood when things are tough.

418. Empower others to make a difference and challenge the process.

419. Don't micro-manage.

420. Don't let the desire to be perfect get in the way of delivering.

421. Be laser focused on people and being an effective communicator.

422. Focus on achieving results.

423. Care about others and be willing to help.

424. Trust others to do their jobs and again, avoid the temptation of micro-managing.

425. Work hard and be dedicated.

426. If you can dream it, you can do it.

427. Don't limit yourself. You go as far as your mind lets you.

428. Nobody is going to hand you anything.

429. It's up to you to chart your own path.

430. If you are going to succeed, you need initiative.

431. Career opportunities should be evaluated for what they are, not where they are.

432. Always treat everyone with dignity and respect.

433. There's no such word as "can't."

434. People will not recognize you unless you stand under the spotlight a little.

435. Balance career, family and health.

436. Engage with people and lead with confidence.

437. Commit to getting the job done.

438. Don't underestimate the value of communication.

439. Over communicate with those that need to understand your message.

440. What gets measured gets managed.

441. Always be on time.

442. Be polite.

443. Treat people the way you want to be treated.

444. Be responsible.

445. Learn from your mistakes.

446. Accept feedback and get better.

447. Provide those around you feedback so they can get better.

448. Get to know the individuals you work with personally. The stronger the relationships are, the stronger the team.

449. Trust your gut and follow your instincts.

450. Lead by example.

451. Be involved with your team.

452. The person you are today has been shaped over time by all those who have been around you.

453. If you say you are going to do something, do it.

454. Policies are created to address routine situations, but special circumstances call for more evaluation and perhaps a deviation from policy.

455. Bullying behavior is not to be admired or emulated.

456. Always treat your customers the way you would like to be treated.

457. Have faith and trust in your workers to do their jobs.

458. When others make a mistake, be quick to support and coach on how to prevent it from happening again.

459. Have a passion for employees and serving customers.

460. Be energetic, optimistic and fun-loving.

461. Be truly interested in knowing each employee as a person.

462. Always look for what is possible.

463. Listen to, groom and provide growth opportunities for employees.

464. Question business decisions to ensure that they are benefitting the customer or the company.

465. Always respect and trust your employees.

466. Provide staff with the right tools and guidance and rest will take care of itself.

467. Take time for yourself, your family and your friends.

468. Always do what you say you are going to do, and if you can't, let the other person know you are not able to do it. Otherwise, you will lose credibility, trust and respect.

469. If you treat your employees well, coach them, encourage them and give them space to grow, the sky is the limit.

470. Getting to know an individual personally is one of the greatest gifts you can give as well as receive.

INDEX

A

B

C

T

CPSIA information can be obtained
at www.ICGtesting.com
Printed in the USA
LVHW041037230119
604882LV00005BA/8/P

9 780996 136044